Political Sociology of Adu

INTERNATIONAL ISSUES IN ADULT EDUCATION

Series Editor:
Peter Mayo, *University of Malta, Msida, Malta*

Editorial Advisory Board:
Stephen Brookfield, University of St Thomas, Minnesota, USA
Waguida El Bakary, American University in Cairo, Egypt
Budd L. Hall, University of Victoria, BC, Canada
Astrid Von Kotze, University of Natal, South Africa
Alberto Melo, University of the Algarve, Portugal
Lidia Puigvert-Mallart, CREA-University of Barcelona, Spain
Daniel Schugurensky, OISE/University of Toronto, Canada
Joyce Stalker, University of Waikato, Hamilton, New Zealand/ Aotearoa
Juha Suoranta, University of Tampere, Finland

Scope:
This international book series attempts to do justice to adult education as an ever expanding field. It is intended to be internationally inclusive and attract writers and readers from different parts of the world. It also attempts to cover many of the areas that feature prominently in this amorphous field. It is a series that seeks to underline the global dimensions of adult education, covering a whole range of perspectives. In this regard, the series seeks to fill in an international void by providing a book series that complements the many journals, professional and academic, that exist in the area. The scope would be broad enough to comprise such issues as 'Adult Education in specific regional contexts', 'Adult Education in the Arab world', 'Participatory Action Research and Adult Education', 'Adult Education and Participatory Citizenship', 'Adult Education and the World Social Forum', 'Adult Education and Disability', 'Adult Education and the Elderly', 'Adult Education in Prisons', 'Adult Education, Work and Livelihoods', 'Adult Education and Migration', 'The Education of Older Adults', 'Southern Perspectives on Adult Education', 'Adult Education and Progressive Social Movements', 'Popular Education in Latin America and Beyond', 'Eastern European perspectives on Adult Education', 'An anti-Racist Agenda in Adult Education', 'Postcolonial perspectives on Adult Education', 'Adult Education and Indigenous Movements', 'Adult Education and Small States'. There is also room for single country studies of Adult Education provided that a market for such a study is guaranteed.

Political Sociology of Adult Education

Carlos Alberto Torres
Paulo Freire Institute
Department of Education-Graduate School of Education and Information Studies
University of California-Los Angeles (UCLA)

SENSE PUBLISHERS
ROTTERDAM/BOSTON/TAIPEI

A C.I.P. record for this book is available from the Library of Congress.

ISBN: 978-94-6209-225-9 (paperback)
ISBN: 978-94-6209-226-6 (hardback)
ISBN: 978-94-6209-227-3 (e-book)

Published by: Sense Publishers,
P.O. Box 21858,
3001 AW Rotterdam,
The Netherlands
https://www.sensepublishers.com/

Printed on acid-free paper

TABLE OF CONTENTS

PREFACE

A SOCIOLOGY OF ADULT EDUCATION

This wide sociological overview of the challenges and prospects for adult education to survive, not necessarily as a form of practice (I do not see any danger here) but as a discipline and area of political inquiry, is a most welcome addition to the series "International Issues in Adult Education." It is welcome for a variety of reasons. In the first place, it is sociological in approach and I have long felt that we need another book-length work in the area of sociology of adult education to build on the initial and still worthy effort, in the mid-eighties, by Peter Jarvis (1985) to open up this space of sociological inquiry. I recall having used Jarvis' book as the main text for a course I taught in the late eighties and early nineties, titled "Sociology of Adult Education," which had represented my baptism as a university teacher. I recall that this text focused on different conceptualizations of adult continuing education, in particular the continuum between "education from above" and "education of equals," the functions (latent and manifest) of adult education, and its relation to social policy. I provided a complementary reading to this text. This was an exploratory paper by Carlos Alberto Torres (1987) outlining an agenda for research in policymaking in adult education. I am thrilled to see that this work constitutes the bedrock for his current manuscript.

This goes to show that the book I am prefacing has many long years behind it in terms of gradual (re)conceptualization and development of the arguments involved. Even then, Torres had been attaching great importance to the role of social movements in adult education. It is safe to declare that the role that these movements have been playing in the development and conceptualization of collective adult learning has not diminished. It has continued to grow and if anything has necessitated a more nuanced and multi-varied analysis of its effects on the adult learning firmament because of its complexity regarding the changing guises of the State, against which these movements must be viewed. What made the body of literature even richer was the gradual international recognition of the contextual differences of the various vibrant movements available, especially those referred to as subaltern Southern social movements (SSSMs), which feature prominently in this book, not least because of Carlos Torres' rooting in his native Latin America, from whence many of the most prominent SSSMs emerged.

It was great to return to the line of inquiry adopted by Torres after all these years. He was one of my mentors in this and related areas (sociology of education and comparative/international education), having taught and co-supervised me at the University of Alberta, when he served as a Killam Fellow while I was pursuing my Master's course in sociology of education. It is thrilling to see how the line of argument laid out in the 1987 occasional paper for the U of A's now defunct

Centre for International Education and Development, directed by the late M. Kazim Bacchus, continued to develop. Torres took on issues related to subsequent world and regional developments, in particular the intensification of globalization and the all-pervasive neoliberal policy blueprints in mainstream adult education policymaking and provision, as well as the different challenges emerging from Latin America, Africa, India, and also Western Europe and North America.

I cannot think of anyone better to provide such a nuanced and genuinely international discussion of the complexities involved than Carlos Alberto Torres. His grounding in comparative education under Martin Carnoy at Stanford University and his far reaching international research and range of contacts in sociological and education research make him the right person for this undertaking. Torres brings both a social theory and a political economy perspective to the field. He does not eschew perhaps too hastily overlooked old theories of the State. As was his style in earlier important works on non-formal education, including his much cited 1990 book on the subject (Torres, 1990), partly a response to an earlier influential book by La Belle (1986), he continues to draw heavily on up-to-date re-conceptualizations of the State, in an age of intensified globalization, as a backdrop to adult education. Much of the groundwork for this would, I presume, have emerged from his excellent discussion on the subject with Maria del Pilar O'Cadiz and Pia Wong in a book on Paulo Freire's school reforms in São Paulo (O'Cadiz et al, 1998). Ever the comparativist, Torres drew on excellent comparative work on popular education in Nicaragua, Cuba, Grenada, and Tanzania, with the works of Robert Arnove and Jeff Unsicker at the foreground, not to mention that of his one-time student, collaborator/co-author and now firmly established scholar, Daniel Schugurensky. But Carlos is a man who strides across different continents from which he draws constant sustenance that continues to strengthen the international reach of his sociological and comparative analysis of education. Latin America co-exists with not only Europe and North America in his analysis, but also with Southeast Asia and the Arab world. This colorful and varied background makes for an internationally rich compendium, a richness which rendered him the prime candidate to write the initial draft of UNESCO's General Report on Adult Learning and Education (GRALE), elements of which are woven throughout this text.

The political economic and international analysis is enriched by constant recourse to some of the finest theorists in the sociological and philosophical fields, something which certainly characterized his earlier work with Raymond A. Morrow (Morrow & Torres, 1995, 2002), but which is also strongly felt throughout this text. For Torres, theory plays an important role in educational analysis and that includes adult education analysis. In this regard, he strikes me as revitalizing an aspect of adult education research badly in need of resuscitation in an area in which there is an obsession with "practice" and an aversion to such theory – with some notable and laudable exceptions of course (e.g. Stephen Brookfield, John Holst, Sallie Westwood, Richard Edwards, John Field, Michael Welton, Andreas Frejes, and the recently deceased Paula Allman, to name but a few). Torres seems to be saying that social theorists, and sophisticated ones at that, are a dying breed in adult education research and he makes every effort to put this right.

And yet, as with the original 1987 occasional paper and one its offshoots, a journal article (Torres, 1991), Torres' regard for theory does not eclipse any concern with policy research. This book provides ample evidence of this as it examines a variety of policy documents, not least those connected with the various adult education congresses from Elsinore to the more recent ones at Hamburg and Belen. These are thoroughly scrutinized for what they bring to or omit from the policy agenda.

I welcome this important addition to adult educational inquiry. I also consider this text to be an important addition to the literature in sociology of education and sociology in general. Adult education remains an important area of inquiry in sociological research and should therefore feature prominently among this larger discipline's sub-fields.

Peter Mayo
Series Editor

REFERENCES

Jarvis, P. (1985). *The Sociology of Adult Continuing Education*, London: Croom Helm.

La Belle, T.J. (1986). *Nonformal education in Latin America and the Caribbean: Stability, reform or revolution?* New York: Praeger.

Morrow, R.A., & Torres, C.A. (1995). *Social theory and education. A critique of theories of social and cultural reproduction*, Albany: SUNY Press.

Morrow, R.A., & Torres, C.A. (2002). *Reading Freire and Habermas: Critical pedagogy and transformative social change.* New York: Teachers' College Press.

O'Cadiz, P., Wong, P.L., & Torres, C.A. (1998). *Education and democracy. Paulo Freire, social movements and educational reform in São Paulo.* Boulder, CO: Westview Press.

Torres, C.A. (1987). Towards a political sociology of adult education. An agenda for research in adult education policymaking. Occasional paper No. 4, Centre for International Education and Development, Department of Educational Foundations, University of Alberta.

Torres, C.A. (1990). *The politics of nonformal education in Latin America.* New York: Praeger.

Torres, C.A. (1991). A political sociology of adult education. A research agenda. *Education* (Malta), *4*(1), 29–34.

INTRODUCTION

"The useful task of the historian is to keep the memory green."

John Kenneth Galbraith[1]

Every twelve years, the UNESCO Institute for Lifelong Learning (UIL) based in Hamburg is responsible for organizing the International Conference on Adult Education (CONFINTEA).[2] In 2009, the then Director of UIL noted that:

> The Sixth International Conference on Adult Education (CONFINTEA VI) was held from 1 to 4 December 2009 in Belém, Brazil, with the participation of over 1,100 delegates, including 55 Ministers and Deputy Ministers from 144 UNESCO Member States. The Conference closed with the adoption of the Belém Framework for Action, which records the commitments of Member States and presents a strategic guide for the global development of adult literacy and adult education within the perspective of lifelong learning. Moreover, CONFINTEA VI saw the launch of the first Global Report on Adult Learning and Education (GRALE). (UNESCO, 2009a)[3]

UNESCO is not the only international organization concerned with adult education, however. Similar to what happened in Hamburg in 1997, for example, when non-governmental organizations were invited as a separate category of representative bodies to CONFINTEA (Hinzen, 2007; Knoll, 2007), many organizations working on adult education met in Belém just before CONFINTEA VI at the International Civil Society Forum (FISC in Portuguese, ICSF in English). The FISC defines itself as:

> A plural, non-denominational, non-governmental and non-partisan space, which is open to diverse identities and individuals, involved in practices of Youth and Adult Education, it promotes the respect of human rights, through the practice of a participatory democracy and a development model that is sustainable and preserves diversity, through egalitarian, solidarity and peaceful relationships among individuals, peoples, and different gender and ethnic groups, condemning all forms of domination and subordination of one human being to another.[4]

The conference's participants exchanged experiences, debated what should be achieved at CONFINTEA VI and how they could contribute to the proceedings, and deliberated what different organizations, communities, and social movements should do to compensate for the lack of state investment in adult education. They also discussed how to correct misguided actions that states undertake and worked on strategies to challenge the ways that adult education is being developed by nation-states worldwide.

One of the key outcomes of the civil society meeting was the affirmation of adult education as a human right, one that is widely guaranteed by national legislatures and, as such, is enforceable through the courts. Another important outcome was the recognition of popular education as a model to develop adult education as a means of social and political transformation. There was consensus throughout the meeting that the institutions of the civil society should play a key role in developing adult education policy, not just governments and their particular priorities.

From the perspective of civil society organizations, adult education should contribute not only to economic development or employment, as most government policies emphasize, but also to the welfare of individuals and communities and to the promotion of a democratic citizenship. One of the conference's strongest recommendations, expressed by representatives of civil society, was that governments should allocate at least 6 percent of their budgets to adult education (Lima, 2010).

The list of partners that came together to organize FISC is truly impressive, a kind of "Who's Who" in international adult education.[5] The dynamism of civil society organizations has reached formidable levels after the crises of capitalism that brought the global economy to its gravest economic depression since 1929, the growing economic and cultural inequity on most continents, and the lack of sensible responses from the ruling elites and nation-states, including their much-discussed solutions to educational crises. It is important to highlight what I called "the Brazilian effect" and the role of social movements challenging neoliberalism.

In this introduction, setting the tone for a discussion of new developments in adult learning education I highlight the antinomies of UNESCO in adult education and lifelong learning. Later in the book I discuss new social movements' use of popular education as a tool for empowerment. CONFINTEA VI's call to move from rhetoric to action demands that we take seriously the agendas of the new social movements in the era of post-neoliberalism.

THE BRAZILIAN 'EFFECT'

"Understanding the limits of educational practice requires political clarity on the part of educators with respect to their project. (...) I cannot recognize the limits of the politico-educative practice in which I am involved if I do not know or if I am not clear about in whose favor I work."[6]

Brazil has long been in the eye of the storm in matters concerning adult learning education, not only because of the legendary figure of Paulo Freire and his unique contributions to adult education or the recent organization of the International Civil Society Forum and the CONFINTEA VI meeting in Amazonia, but also because one of the most noteworthy social movement initiatives took place in Southern Brazil in the city of Porto Alegre, Rio Grande do Sul. Porto Alegre is also known for its experiences with participatory budgeting planning and "thick" democratic and participative models of governance (Daly, Schugurensky, & Lopes, 2009).

A decade ago a new beginning for social movements worldwide took place with the inception of the World Social Forum (WSF) challenging the hegemony of the World Economic Forum (WEF) that is celebrated every winter in Davos, Switzerland.

The original Davos meeting was organized in January 1971 by the European Union and European Professional Associations as a European Management Forum. After the collapse of the Bretton-Woods fixed-exchange-rate mechanism and other challenging world events such as the Arab-Israeli war, the Forum quickly expanded its focus from management to social, economic, and political issues. In 1987 it changed its name to the World Economic Forum.

To counteract the influence of the WEF and to help promote global anti-hegemonic strategies developed by a growing number of social movements concerned about the effects of neoliberal globalization, the World Social Forum (WSF) was born.

The WSF has grown over the past decade as a result of increasing awareness of and resistance to globalization and neoliberalism. Perhaps it was simply a coincidence in timing, but in February 2010, shortly after CONFINTEA VI had ended in December 2009, the World Social Forum (WSF) celebrated its tenth anniversary in the presence of hundreds of social movements and community organizations as well as critical intellectuals and political leaders.

The principal speaker was Brazilian President Luiz Inácio Lula da Silva. The paradox is that Lula, one of the original founders of the World Social Forum as a union leader and then as leader of the Partido dos Trabalhadores (Workers' Party), spoke at the WSF meeting on his way to the World Economic Forum to receive an award for his stewardship during the deep economic crisis, when he served as an example of statesmanship to the rest of the world. Time magazine also recognized President Lula as the most influential world leader in 2010.

There is a rich and growing bibliography on the World Social Forum and its contributions to social, political, and economic policies. It is pertinent to cite at length Milani and Laniado's (2006) conclusion about the World Social Forum:

> The World Social Forum is a relevant open-space movement precisely because it contrasts with the formalist self referred political system of representative democracy and traditional international relations. The social and political orders (national and international) of modern societies have been observed as balanced structures that have supposedly contemplated a predictable and universal material progress and a class society based on interests and a general sense of citizenship. The new social movements and later the transnational movements question the democracy deficit and the ineffectiveness of international regulation of world politics which have resulted from this received model of society. Globalization forces the emergence of strong paradoxes of both contemporary democracy and the asymmetric international relations. It uncovers the enormous cleavage between an idealized progress promised by liberal Keynesian democracy (not to speak of socialist experiences) and the limited institutional capacity to guarantee liberty and to provide equality

worldwide and within the principle of justice. Consequently, the transnational social movements have played an important role by exposing the disconnections between liberty, distribution and recognition. (p. 31)

As an emblematic forum and network, the WSF is exemplary of the way that new social movements have challenged the hegemony of neoliberal governance (Gadotti, 2010; Milani and Laniado, 2006; Torres, 2009b). What is not well studied is how this process is related to adult learning education. While this book will offer some insights to this extent, it is by no means an analysis of the complex relationship between social movements and adult learning education, which is subject for another research.

In thinking about the new policy orientations that CONFINTEA VI tried to spark, as well as the need for a renewed commitment to adult education and lifelong learning, it will be useful to explore briefly the experience of social movements confronting neoliberalism in Latin America and the implications for adult education. This will be done in several sections of this book.

THIS BOOK

More than 20 years ago, I published a book that was translated into several languages and used as a textbook in many departments and schools of education in the world, particularly in those places where a concern about adult learning education and nonformal education was paramount. This book, entitled *The Politics of Non-Formal Education in Latin America,* was a first attempt to develop a political sociology of adult education.

A political sociology of education is an interdisciplinary hybrid. As I have argued, it aims to study power and relations of authority in education, and the political underpinnings and implications of educational policies: It suggests an analytical approach concerned with the connections among religion, kinship relations, social classes, interest groups (of the most diverse type), and the political culture (ideology, value system, *weltanschauung*) of actors and social groups in the determination of political decisions and in the constitution of social consensus — or, failing that, a confrontation or distancing — of actors and social classes with respect to the legitimation of public policy. Obviously, any study in political sociology has to consider questions of bureaucracy and rationalization, power, influence, authority, and the constitutive aspects of such social interactions (clients and political and social actors, their perceptions of the fundamental questions of political conflict, and the alternative programs that derive from these). Similarly, at the heart of a political sociology are the connections between civil and political society, as well as the complex interactions among individual subjects, collective subjects, and social practices. A political sociology of education implies considering all of these topics, theoretical questions, and problematics in a specific program of investigation to understand why a given educational policy is created; how it is planned, constructed, and implemented; who are the most relevant actors in its formulation and operationalization; what are the repercussions of such policy for both its clienteles and its social questions; and what are the fundamental, systemic, and organizational processes involved from its origins to the implementation and evaluation of the policy (Torres, 1990c, p. xvii).

A political sociology of education has marked features including its structural historical analysis focus; its emphasis on the political raison d être of educational practices and policies; its reliance on theories of the state as a theoretical backbone; its critique of instrumental rationalization as the only feasible, practical, and cost-effective way to adequate means to ends; its focus on the politicity of education and educational policy formation as its theoretical and practical leitmotif; its concern for multicentered (but not decentered) notions of power (and hence interest and privilege); and finally the attempt to frame the research questions, theoretical rationale, and policy implications in terms of the importance of ideology and the scholarship of class, race, gender, and the state in comparative perspective (Torres, 2009b, p. 122).

Despite its impact on the field at the time, what I discussed in *The Politics of Nonformal Education* has become a piece of social history of thought and action in adult learning education. While the analysis is by no means obsolete, it has become evident to me that in the context of new developments in adult learning education, particularly the impact of globalization, neoliberalism, and the new role of international organizations in reconceptualizing lifelong learning, new evidence-based research, new narratives, and new theoretical designs are needed. Hence this book which offers a political sociology of adult learning education, with a critical perspective based on Critical Social Theory and the always inspiring work of Paulo Freire.

For critical theorists, research cannot be separated from political struggle. But are scholarship and activism inevitably part and parcel of our life journey? Paulo Freire argued that politics and education could not be easily separated. The same applies to scholarship and political struggle. They cannot be easily dissociated, not even for purely didactic purposes. Conducting research and teaching to change the world is not simply observing what happens around us as detached scientists. Critical scholars do not share with their technocrat counterparts the illusion that manipulating knowledge, using technocratic means, and the stern application of instrumental rationality will solve most if not all of education's ills.

The first chapter discusses some of the premises embedded in reconceptualizing lifelong learning. The second chapter uses the tools of the political sociology of adult learning education to explore some of the main orientations in the field. The third chapter discusses critically the prevailing rationales in adult learning education. The fourth chapter confronts the limits and possibilities of adult learning education facing the civilization crises that we are experiencing at the beginning of the twenty first century. The fifth chapter, with a title that is both provocative and evocative of the history of the field, "Reinventing Adult Learning Education: Unleashing the

Power, Reclaiming the Dream," attempts to look at the complex issues, limits and possibilities when adult learning education is discussed not only in the complexity of its theories and data, but also as a form of advocacy for social justice education. The sixth chapter provides an analysis of adult learning education and literacy in an international comparative perspective. Finally, the seventh chapter provides a systematic analysis of the role of Critical Theory and public intellectuals.

NOTES

1   Galbraith, J. K. (1954). *The great crash of 1929*. Cambridge, Houghton Mifflin Co, p. xx.
2   Excerpts of an article by Carlos Alberto Torres entitled "Dancing on the Deck of the Titanic? Adult Education, the Nation-State, and New Social Movements" [Article published in the *International Review of Education*, Special Issue on CONFINTEA and its role in sustaining the plight of adult learning and education. Guest Editors, Carolyn Medel Añonuevo, Richard DeJardins, and Carlos Alberto Torres] International Review of Education, (2011) 57, pages 39–55. Reproduced with authorization.
3   Public letter sent after the CONFINTEA VI.
4   For more on the International Civil Society Forum, see http://www.fisc2009.org/eng/index.php?option=com_content&view=article&id=17&Itemid=2
5   The organization of the FISC was the product of several partners, a kind of "Who's Who" of adult learning education in the global civil society. The International Committee included Ação Educativa, the Asian South Pacific Bureau of Adult Education (ASPBAE), the Latin American Council for Adult Education (CEAAL) the Latin American Campaign for the Right to Education (CLADE), the International Council of Adult Education (ICAE), and the African Platform/La Plataforme Africaine/A Plataforma Africana. The Organizing Committee in Brazil included the National Campaign for the Right to Education, the National Confederation of Agriculture Workers (CONTAG), the Workers' Union (CUT), MOVA Forum, the Paulo Freire Institute, the Landless Movement (MST), the Popular Education Network of Women from Latin America and the Caribbean, and the Fórum EJA Paulista. The Local Organizing Committee included the Associação Paraense de Apoio ás Comunidades Carentes (APACC), the Associação Regional das Casas Familiares Rurais do Pará (ARCAFAR), the State Council of Education (CEE), Centro de Defensa do Negro do Pará (CEDENPA), Commission for the Pan-Amazonia, DETRAN/PA, Empresa de Assisténsia Técnica e Extensão Rural do Pará (EMATER), Facultade de Amazónia (FAMA), Fórum da Amazónia Oriental (FAOR), Fórum EJA Pará, Fórum Paraense de Economia Solidária, Fórum Paraense de Educação do Campo (FPEC), Instituto Federal do Pará (IFPA), Grupo de Mulheres da Area Central (GEMPAC), Instituto Amazónia Solidária e Sustentável (IAMAS), Instituto Saber Ser Amazónia Ribeirinha (ISSAR). Núcleo de Educação Paulo Freire/NEP-UEPA, Rede de Educação Cidadã) (RECID), Rede Cidadania Solidária, Secretary of Education of the State of Pará (SEDUC), Secretary of Government (SEGOV), Sindicato Nacional dos Servidores Federais da Educação Básica, Profissional e Tecnológica, Sindicato dos Pedagogos, University of the State of Pará (UEPA), Federal University of Pará (UFPA), Federal University of Amapá (UNIFAP), Institute Popular University (UNIPOP). And there were a host of other supportrs, including the African Newtwork Campaign on Education for All (ANCEFA), the Arab Network for Literacy and Adult Education, (ANLAE), the Caribbean Regional Council of Adult Education (CARCAE), the European Association for Education of Adults (EAEA), the African Women's Development and Communication Network (FEMNET), the North American Alliance for Popular and Adult Education (NAPAAE), the Pan African Association for Literacy and Adult Education (PALAAE), and the Africa Reflect Network (PAMOJA).
6   Freire, P. (1998). *Politics and Education*, Los Angeles, UCLA Latin American Center Publications — translated by Pia Lindquist Wong, with an introduction entitled "The Political Pedagogy of Paulo Freire" by Carlos Alberto Torres, p. 46.

CHAPTER I

RECONCEPTUALIZING LIFELONG LEARNING[1]

"The only absolutely certain thing is the future, since the past is constantly changing."[2]

For the UNESCO Lifelong Learning Institute, coordinating and writing the General Report on Adult Learning Education (GRALE report) was not an easy feat. Like many documents of its kind, GRALE is a policy advocacy document, drawing from reports produced by governments, secondary data, and supplementary empirical reports and information. Yet to have the academic and political credibility, it should have been influenced by state of the art debates in the field of adult and lifelong learning, a field that is rather under-theorized.

Clearly, any portrait that describes and analyzes the narratives of policymakers and other stakeholders, adult learning education's policy orientation, values philosophy, legislation, financing strategy, or governance, could be subject to a critique. As Desjardins (2008) aptly argues:

> There are at least two major trends surrounding adult education which have intensified in recent years. The first involves the phenomenon of globalization and the accompanying transnationalization of education policy making which has a number of implications for policy studies. The second involves a renewed pressure for strategic and policy relevant research. The two are related but they bring forth different sets of issues that pertain to the field of adult education and also the need for different responses. (p. 1)

Any policy advocacy document reminds us that there is a tension between the sense of urgency and pragmatism based on bureaucratic and political underpinnings affecting the technical and administrative domains of the public sectors, and the more "removed" or "detached" – and yet poignant and relevant – analysis and critique from academia. The world of academia and the world of the public sector are two distinct words, and they eventually – but not very easily because of a number of conflicting interest and ethical issues – may intersect.

These two worlds could be defined in terms of Habermas's dichotomy of social action. Social action can be either success-oriented strategic action or understanding-oriented communicative action. According to Habermas, non-social action is always purposive-rational instrumental action: the actor makes use of specific objects for his or her own social benefit. "Strategic action is purposive-rational action oriented towards other persons from a utilitarian point of view. The actor does not treat others as genuine persons, rather as natural objects. Strategic action means calculative exploitation, or manipulation, of others" (Habermas, 1984, pp. 285, 333; Huttunen, 2008).

One of the most difficult, and yet possible, tasks is to find ways to create synergy between these two worlds and a cross-pollination of ideas, praxis, values, orientations, priorities, and goals. Methodologically and theoretically there are serious obstacles to accomplish these type of report, considering the tensions between "evidence-based research" (OECD, 2007) and qualitative narrative strategies:

> We find the tension between 'evidence- based' research which tends to tell us a story as long as it is based on some statistical analysis considered the truth of the matter, and the more qualitative, narrative oriented stories that come from lived experience and in many respects are profoundly autobiographical (Burke & Jackson, p. 2).

Despite this tension, evidence-based research, based on methodological pluralism, continues to be a great challenge for scientists as much as for journalists. Examples of the need for serious empirical inquiry abound even in the convoluted world of political competition and intrigue.[3]

It should not be a surprise that when we scratch a theory we find a biography. (Torres, 1998). When we talk about "life," we do not talk just about socially constructed facts that give some pleasure and solace to statisticians, mathematicians or a great number of people who look at the world as voyeurs. We talk about lived experience. In their book *Reconceptualizing Lifelong Learning: Feminist Interventions*, Penny Jane Burke and Sue Jackson argued:

> We challenge definitions of 'evidence-based' research which rely on quantitative data as though it somehow speaks 'the truth.' Whilst quantitative data can be useful, it does not — cannot — tell a complete story; a story needs a narrative. The narrative always of course belongs to the researcher, the storyteller, although it is differently experienced by its audiences. (Burke & Jackson, 2007, p. 2)

There is much more out there besides evidence-based research that deserves to be considered, listened to, and incorporated into a document of policy advocacy, let alone into educational research.

As I argue in this chapter, the terminology of the field is subject to much controversy and needs to be retooled carefully. Taking a meta-theoretical perspective, it is important to emphasize that in our lifelong learning conceptualizations we actually address three key terms: "life," "long," and "learning."

The conceptualization of lifelong learning is part of hegemonic discourses, which are classed and racialized, as well as gendered. The emphasis on instrumental, technical, and mechanical sets of skills, outcomes, and competencies tend to follow "neoliberal constructions of lifelong learning embedded in a hierarchical individualism" (Burke & Jackson, 2007, p. 2).

Thus, in the context of this book, I critically discuss globalization and neoliberalism as social-historical processes and political-pedagogic processes, impacting and eventually guiding research agendas, cognizant of the fact that "discourse and policy, is often used more as an agent of social control than as an agent for change and transformative action" (Burke & Jackson, 2007, p. 10). After all, as feminist philosopher Judith Butler reminds us, social and political critique is at the core of ethical action (Butler, 2005).

There is a conceptual and practical tension between lifelong learning and lifelong education. Yet, any reconceptualization of lifelong learning should acknowledge an important shift in the educational discourse of the past two or three decades, a move from "education" to "learning." Hence the focus has shifted from teacher to learner, and from formal to nonformal and informal learning experiences, within and outside of educational institutions, within the workplace and given the virtuality of the new cybernetic culture, virtually everywhere.

The "learning" part of the story is also a new development, through not necessarily fully incorporated or practiced everywhere. Traditionally it has had a dominant presence in European discussions, for instance, but has been less important in the conversation in Latin America.

Finally, the "long" part of the concept matters. When learning becomes lifelong, we move away from a period of time in the life of an individual, and we also move away from a set of clearly defined particular institutions imparting such education and facilitating such learning.

Not only do we address the notion of a continuum in the learning activities that we engage in, but we also enhance the domains of learning from instrumental to self-reflexive learning, and from belonging to identity, addressing the crucial political philosophical distinction between individualization and community building. Reflecting a process that naturally creates a set of tensions and contradictions in a central component of Western political philosophy, there is the need to affirm simultaneously the individuality of people in their own right, without denying and in fact reaffirming the importance of the community and its own legacies and virtues.

Lifelong learning as a paradigm addresses also some of the most pressing needs of human beings, including personal growth and development, improved health and well-being, and explicitly linking learning and education to labor skills and employment, competition in a global economy, and innovation and the knowledge society as new factors of production. Yet the concept is so all encompassing that it also includes contributions to technological and digital development, intercultural and linguistic relations, ageing populations and their life choices (public as well as private) for the so-called "Third Age." Finally, the concept addresses the core of political socialization, participation and integration of civil societies and democratic governance, including the challenges of immigration, multiculturalism and affirmative action.

If one considers the array of learning responsibilities and learning outcomes included in the concept, that is, knowledge, skills and wider competencies, one may wonder what exactly falls outside the concept of lifelong learning beyond the educational and learning experiences of childhood?

The problems of defining the object of study and the problems of conceptualization as well as the analytical normative and pragmatic definitions will emerge in the following chapters, showing that there is a problem of identity in the field of adult learning education, a field representing a spectrum of meanings and commitments.

The "elusiveness," complexity, and heterogeneity of the object of study will require serious reflection and analysis of conceptual and terminological issues. This conceptual conundrum is conflated by the tensions between national and supra-national experiences in adult learning education, and global-local, and local-local tensions in the world system:

> Because adult learning education policies and practices are essentially national, a wide range of factors contribute to the condition of ALE in any country including: the prevailing socio-political culture comprising beliefs and values about the role of the state in general and in relation to education and training in particular; prevailing views on the function of education and training – in this, case ALE – in relation to the social, cultural, political and economic goals and priorities of a country; the dominant views on the optimal balance of power, roles and activity between the three major social institutions, state, market, and civil society; the systems of ALE governance in operation, including the role of the social partners; the level of economic development and the level of investment in education and training. (Keogh, 2008, pp. 45–47)

Another grey area pertains to the foundations of adult learning education as lifelong learning curricula. Drawing from the theoretical reservoir of Critical Theory, and particularly the work of Paulo Freire, I shall provide a lengthy discussion of some of the foundational principles for a renewed vision of adult learning education as a paradigm, including how Critical Theory can contribute to the field and to the role of public intellectuals reinvigorating the field.

NOTES

[1] Time and again, individuals and institutions build conceptual constructs, which are really social constructs, modifying over time specific debates, fields, and policies. Such constructs are presented throughout this book, and occasionally I refer to them as interchangeable. I refer to adult education, a concept traditionally used in the second half of the twentieth century; adult learning education, a new terminology adopted by UNESCO in the past two or three decades to incorporate the question of learning; lifelong learning, which supplements some of the key discussions about learning through life; and other concepts. This is not the place to undertake a definitional discussion of terms, concepts, and social constructions. I am not sure how useful such a discussion is, and feel that it eventually could detract from the key issues of a political sociology of education.

[2] A Yugoslavian aphorism cited by Immanuel Wallerstein in "A Left Politics for the 21st Century? or, Theory and Praxis Once Again" in *Democratie*, Fernand Braudel Center, University of New York, Binghamton, 1999, p. 1.

[3] The flap over "Joe the Plumber" during debates between presidential candidates John McCain and Barack Obama in the 2008 U.S. election is telling of the importance that narratives play in politics. There is no question that seriously informed narratives should also play a key role in policy documents. While both camps were competing for recognition of their own proposals for changes in

the administration and governance of the United States, in the last debate Senator McCain quoted or cited several times the exchanges between Senator Obama and "Joe the Plumber" during a campaign stop in Ohio, a swing state, to prove that Senator's Obama economic proposal would damage the hard-working middle class. It seems that in a time of crisis it is better to put a human face on a situation than to rely solely on evidence-based research built on cold statistics. Of course we need some sort of fact-finding or evidence-based research because "Joe the Plumber" catapulted to fame overnight, becoming the subject of frantic research by journalists. He turned out to be an individual who didn't have a plumber's license, made only $40,000 a year, and was hence incapable of buying, as he claimed he would attempt to do, the company he worked for. Finally, he had not paid taxes to the IRS for many years! Yet in the context of spectacle democracies, as we experience in this period of late capitalism, after the election, "Joe the Plumber" tried to start a political career in the Republican party.

A POLITICAL SOCIOLOGY OF ADULT LEARNING EDUCATION IN THE TWENTY FIRST CENTURY

This chapter offers a political sociology of adult learning education taken to a very holistic and practical analytical level. The arguments are deeply theoretical but also provide a historical-structural analysis. It is written with the belief that it is possible to link the normative principles which UNESCO's GRALE report advocates with the concrete changes in the model of globalization we are experimenting and the responses to the global changes after the financial meltdown of September-October 2008. In doing so, we may be able to move towards new principles of understanding, and taking advantage of the state of the art of specialized knowledge and research, we may be able to offer a useful analytical, normative and pragmatic agenda.

However it is clear that we will be talking about the value-added aspect of adult learning education policies: from policies of employability (a favorite of governments and economists but also unions) to policies of enhancing healthy lifestyles, preventing illnesses, securing better models of development with a strong sustainability approach, apprenticeship programs, better and more caring forms of community action, literacy at several levels (functional, technological, etc.) and knowledge/skills for a society of knowledge.

Adult learning education is today also covering the field of personal development, which is now exemplified usually outside the control of governments in the explosion of "self-help" educational models. There are a lot of for-profit orientations, which are simply merchandizing, but there are also a lot of new spiritual activities (consider for instance the philosophy of Ken Wilber).[1]

Likewise, and connected to the points below, there are extraordinary new initiatives, particularly in the industrial advanced societies, of "conscious capitalism," which provides us with a set of principles that apply to adult learning education.[2] Likewise, there are other areas that could enhance the claim for a new role for adult learning education, like the notion of responsible capitalism, which offers new avenues for green business and the like.[3] Any intelligent reader of these proposals will agree that they cannot be done without a substantive and clever adult learning education orientation or policy model all over the planet.

MAPPING KEY CONCEPTS: GLOBALIZATION, THE LEARNING SOCIETY,
THE KNOWLEDGE-BASED SOCIETY AND THE NETWORK SOCIETY

"Maybe we have enjoyed our present democratic freedom so much that we are passionately dreaming about it. However, this taste and this passion for freedom coexist with authoritarian traditions and practices, resulting in one of our ambiguities."[4]

What follows is a brief excursus mapping the elusiveness of concepts, which, in the best of the critical modernist tradition, are considered sliding signifiers. Any heuristical analysis of terms such as learning society, knowledge-based/economy, network society or globalization, should trace the origins of the term to a particular document or author. For instance, economist Theodore Levitt is credited with coining the term "globalization" in 1985 to describe changes in global economics affecting production, consumption, and investment (Stromquist, 2002, pp. 19–20). The term quickly has become a favorite catchphrase in the world of business and social sciences, appearing to demonstrate that international exchanges are affecting in many forms the way large segments of the world's population work, live, and relate to culture, education, and apparently everything else.

The term, denoting in a particular way the transformation of capitalism as a mode of production, prompted a group of distinguished European scholars to create in 2003 the journal *Globalization, Societies and Education* and the thematic network Globalization, Europeanization Network in Education (GENIE), both coordinated by professors Roger Dale and Susan Robertson, who have argued that "formal education is the most commonly found institution and most commonly shared experience of all in the contemporary world" (Dale & Robertson, 2003, p. 7).

Globalization is seen as blurring national boundaries, shifting solidarities within and between nation-states, and deeply affecting the constitutions of national and interest-groups identities. What is new is not so much its form as its scale. Since the Bretton Woods conference in 1944, in which the International Monetary Fund and the World Bank were founded, national trade barriers have been eroded, and global economic forces have played a more significant role in local economies. In the six and a half decades that followed that event, international trade has expanded approximately twelve times and foreign direct investment has expanded at two or three times the rate of trade investment (Burbules & Torres, 2000; Mander & Goldsmith, 1996).

Some analysts have argued that we are witnessing the corporatization of the world, rather than simply its globalization (Burbach, 2001; Burbules & Torres, 2000; Kellner, 2000; Rhoads and Szelényi, 2011; Slaughter & Leslie, 1997; Went, 2000). Additionally, globalization has been defined as "the intensification of worldwide social relations which link distant localities in such a way that local happenings are shaped by events occurring many miles away and vice versa" (Held, 1991, p. 9).

David Held suggests among other things, that globalization is the product of the emergence of a global economy, an expansion of transnational linkages between economic units creating new forms of collective decision-making, development of intergovernmental and quasi-supranational institutions, an intensification of transnational communications and the creation of new regional and military orders. Regarding education a critic of neoliberal globalization argues that "the globally structured agenda is defined above all having as a nerve center the great international statistics projects and, in particular, the INES project of the Center for Educational Research and Innovation (CERI) of the OECD" (Teodoro, 2003, p. 198).

Despite its popularity and ever reaching nature, globalization as a historical process homogenizes as much as it fragments societies. That is to say, there is integration but also contestation across cultures (Burbules & Torres, 2000; Carnoy, 1999; Luke & Luke, 2000; Scott, 1998; Torres, 1998a; Urry, 1998).

Dutch sociologist and University of Twente communication professor Jan van Dijk is credited with coining the term "network society" in his book *The Network Society,* originally published in Dutch in 1991. Yet it was the monumental work of Spanish sociologist Manuel Castells in *The Network Society*, the first part of his trilogy *The Information Age* (1996) that catapulted the term to an international currency (Castells, 1996, 1997, 1998).

A network society comprises a combination of social and media networks, giving shape to its prime mode of organization and most important structures at all levels (individual, organizational, and societal). People interact, live, trade, produce, consume, and communicate in networks, which are digital, physical, and virtual (Torres, Romão, & Teodoro, 2012).

The "learning society" is an aspect of this movement to look beyond the formal learning society, locating learning as not just a quality of individuals but also as an element of systems. It is recognized by most educators that the publication of *Learning to Be* by Edgar Faure and collaborators in 1972 constituted a watershed, a humanist educational manifesto of the twentieth century, and marked with distinction the work UNESCO had been doing since its inception in the world system. In its preamble the document expressed the fear of dehumanization, and one of its main messages was that education should enable each person "to be able to solve his own problems, make his own decisions and shoulder his own responsibilities." This initiative of UNESCO, with the publication of *Learning to Be*, brought the concept of a learning society to the forefront of academic and political discussions:

> If learning involves all of one's life, in the sense of both time-span and diversity, and all of society, including its social and economic as well as its educational resources, then we must go even further than the necessary overhaul of 'educational systems' until we reach the stage of a learning society. (Faure, 1972, p. xxxiii)

To unleash the power of adult education to reach new stages of a learning society and increase the humanization of culture and nature seemed "natural" at the time.

Adult Learning Education Paradigms

Adult education paradigms reflect the logic of organization of adult educational services by governments and/or institutions of civil society (NGOs, community organizations, social movements). A great deal of the history of adult education is reflected in terms of its contributions to development and social transformation. For more than seven decades since the creation of UNESCO, adult education has been a key social policy, particularly in less developed countries. It is possible to illuminate the traditions by distinguishing between two strategies of development (incrementalism versus structuralism) and two strategies of political participation (active political participation versus controlled political participation). Hence four alternative modes of policy planning in adult education have emerged over the years:

Table 1. Alternative models of adult education

Political Participation	Incrementalism	Structuralism
Active Political Participation	Modernization-Human Capital	Pedagogy of the Oppressed-Popular Education
Political Control, Limited Participation	Pragmatism Idealism	Social Engineering (Corporatism)

Modernization and human capital theories see adult education as a key variable in the process of economic growth and modernization of traditional societies. The central concept is the notion of the "modern individual" (Inkeles & Smith, 1974). Adult education, and in particular literacy training, contribute to economic and political development of modern societies. They increase the productivity of the newly educated; increase the productivity of those who work with the newly educated; expand the diffusion of useful knowledge to all individuals (with concrete results in health care and child nutrition) while simultaneously reducing the cost of teaching practical information; stimulate the demand for technical training and professional education; act as a means of selecting the most able individuals enhancing their occupational mobility in the economic active population; and reinforce the economic incentives, that is the ability of people to respond positively to any increase in the reward for their efforts (Blaug, 1966).

Politically, social scientists have estimated that adult education and literacy training are preconditions to increase per capita income in developed and developing societies, as well as for producing a democratic civic culture, exposing people to means of mass communication and urbanization, as well as planned and orderly social mobilization of the citizenship (Deutch, 1963; Huntington, 1971; Lerner, 1958; UNESCO, 1968a, 1968b). Finally, an increase in the education of the population is considered intimately related to an increase in equity and equality in the social distribution of goods and services, as well as to an increase in upward social mobility, lowering of rates of fertility and improvement in health indicators (Marin & Psacharopoulos, 1976; Psacharopoulos, 1988). Likewise, adult education plays a major role in value transformation: modernization processes need a substantial change of values (from traditional to modern values) and a modification of individual socio-psychological values increasing traits of individual autonomy facing family traditions, new interest in planning, and a modern sense of efficiency (Lerner, 1958; Shuman, Inkeles & Smith, 1967).

Pedagogy of the Oppressed and popular education see adult education projects as mechanisms for the political and pedagogical empowerment of subordinate social sectors. As pedagogy for social transition, *Pedagogy of the Oppressed* is related to the work of Brazilian pedagogue Paulo Reglus Neves Freire and a number of other educators. They conceive of education as a "cultural act," and a model of consciousness raising for empowerment (Barreiro, 1974; Freire, 1968, 1997). As an anti-authoritarian pedagogy, *Pedagogy of the Oppressed* considers teaching and learning as a two-way process, where the teacher is a student, and the student is also a teacher through a horizontal relationship (Jarvis, 1985; Shor and Freire, 1987; Torres, 2009b). Sharing of the experience, and starting from the knowledge of the students is a liberatory experience, a precondition for consciousness raising. Popular education has an old tradition, reflected for instance in the educational activities of the Workers' Educational Association (WEA), which was founded in 1903 and today is the UK's largest voluntary provider of adult education (Jenning, 2002) Popular education has come to be associated with *Pedagogy of the Oppressed* (Puiggrós, 1984, 2005). It has been practiced in a number of literacy training campaigns, as well as community education (Guinea Bissau, Grenada, Mexico, Brazil, Tanzania, Nicaragua, Chile, Cuba). A seminal point of popular education is to start from the needs and demands of communities rather than from top-down approaches to promote modernization processes. Adult education is seen as closely aligned with popular education as an educational practice, since adult education is closely linked to the needs of communities. It is often practiced through small-scale educational projects designed, promoted, financed, and carried out by NGOs, community organizations, and social movements. Furthermore, the results of adult education are more immediate than formal schooling — which takes 12–15 years of educating children and youth to pay off in the markets — thus, adult learning education may quickly facilitate insertion in labor markets. Models of popular education became well known in the sixties and have continued to challenge established structures, sometimes questioning state programs, and eventually filling in for lack of government programs in poor or marginal communities (Arnove, 1986; La Belle, 1986; Latapí, 1984; Rodriguez Brandão, 1984).

Adult education programs inspired by popular education begin with an analysis of the social and living conditions of the people and their main problems (unemployment, violence, malnutrition, health, etc.), trying to reach a level of collective and individual consciousness of these problems. These models take very seriously the previous knowledge of the individuals, families, and communities involved in the educational and learning process. Rather than simply focusing on a set of abilities, dexterities, knowledge or capacities, these projects also focus on increasing a sense of dignity, self-worth, and personal pride in the participants while addressing their most individual and community pressing problems. Finally, as pedagogical and institutional projects they can be started by governments or community organizations and social movements, they can be directed toward children, youth and adults, and they can be connected with models of integrated rural development and urban marginal groups, along with cooperative production, employment and collective development, and development of civil minimums in solidarity (Arnove, 1986; Razeto, 1990, 2003).

The variety of projects in this paradigm are astonishing: they relate to indigenous populations, questions of language and bilingualism, multiculturalism and interculturalism, revaluation and restoration of identity resisting assimilation with dominant or global cultures; projects linked to participatory action research, a new model of interactive research that has received commensurable legitimacy in academic environments; and projects connected to recuperating collective memories, popular knowledge of under-privileged populations, traditional technologies which preserve the environment, indigenous forms of communication and representation (Chiapas and the diverse projects sponsored by the Zapatista movement); community projects seeking active participation and citizenship; projects connected with agrarian reforms, better use of resources and land holdings, and rural education seeking to empower poor and destitute populations; political projects connecting literary training with political mobilization in defense of specific interests; and contestation activities, or projects of popular education linked to higher education institutions — for instance the Popular Education Alliance in the area of Chicago, Illinois, or the resource library for popular education.[5]

Pragmatic idealism is a key international model that has emerged over the years connected with the contributions of *Learning to Be*, or the Faure Commission Report, and dovetails nicely with some of the premises of U.S. educator John Dewey, as well as other adult education models known as andragogy (Knowles, 1980). One could argue that some of the new contributions emanating from UNESCO's work in the nineties and beginning of the twentieth century, though meta-theoretically different from the more humanistic approach of *Learning to Be*, could be classified under this label.

Following the key premises of Dewey, education and democracy should be intimately related through the formation of moral education as the pivot of development. Adult learning education is an exercise based on experience, and should provide an intimate satisfaction as much as a practical external outcome. From this perspective, several of the key elements associated with democratic education and the practice of human rights in education have been advanced. These include the notion that education is a right and a good that individuals cannot renounce, thus adult education assumes the character of a moral imperative for all individuals, particularly those who are disenfranchised, impoverished, marginalized, or unable to reach the heights of a given culture. Thus, since there is a sense of "deficit," adult education should play a compensatory role, to repair the deficits of learning and access to the premises of the national culture, particularly for individuals who dropped out or never reached full participation in the formal school system. While there may not be substantial differences in the premises of educating children from educating youth and adults, illiteracy continues to be a central problem to be solved, as a "medusa of many heads;" there is a strong emphasis on formal modes of literacy training and adult learning education with teachers and/or adult education learning facilitators playing a most serious role in guaranteeing the quality of educational service and provision. These models of adult education tend to be certified by formal establishments. However, the premise of "learning to be" is the notion of continuing education, or what has been lately termed lifelong learning — from cradle to grave, including learning to do, learning to be together, and learning to know (Coombs, 1968; Faure, the Jacques Delors Commission in its different periods).

Thus education is a continuum: it includes a spatial continuity (does not start and/or end in schools spaces), and it can take place in trade unions, clubs, cultural circles, community organizations, etc; it includes a continuum of learning (from learning to be, to learning to do, to learning to know, to learning to live together, to learning to protect the environment, to learning to transform citizenship); it includes an organic-structural continuum, from the academic to non-academic learning; it includes a vital continuum, from what we learn in schools to what we learn in life; it includes a continuum in communication, from what we learn at home, at church, or at school, to what we learn through mass media or informal exchanges (Furter, 1966a, 1966b; Torres, 1990a, 2009a).

Thus lifelong learning appears as a cultural strategy in the process of integral and holistic development. The role of international and bilateral organizations to achieve these outcomes at global levels is paramount. A learning society is a premise for a knowledge society. Organizational analysis speaks of learning organizations, a central component of the knowledge society and knowledge economy. The idea that knowledge becomes a third productive factor, jointly with capital and labor is the essence of the notion of the knowledge society. UNESCO and other international and multinational organizations have been playing around with the implications of this concept for culture and education (UNESCO, 2005) The notion of knowledge society/knowledge economy, sometimes defined, as an information society has been aptly defined in the Declaration of Lisbon, stating the strategy for the development of higher education in EUA.

The strategy of Lisbon argues that the central task of EU higher education is "to equip Europe's population—young and old—to play their part within the knowledge society, in which economic, social and cultural development depend primarily on the creation and dissemination of knowledge and skills. Modern societies, much more than the agricultural and manufacturing societies of past centuries depend on the application of knowledge, high-level skills, entrepreneurial acumen and the exploitation of communication and information technologies" (Lisbon Declaration, 2005).

Social Engineering (Corporatism) Adult education as social engineering or corporatism conceives of education as primordially an exercise of social engineering in a post-industrial society, where there is a bureaucratic rationality that will make all social distinctions and differences (particularly social class differences) disappear or become irrelevant for social practices. An elite, be it bureaucratic, technical, professional, or scientific, will play a central role in conceiving a model of social planning that will solve ideological and political differences among many strata in the population, creating a scientific and objective rationality of planning and action. From a political theory analysis, there is a sense of "organicism" in this perspective, focusing on decentralized yet controlled political participation of semi-autonomous groups. There is a pyramidal network of interactions, with the state playing a fundamental role in the strategic model of development, articulating diverse interests (e.g. business and working class interest, for instance) with the state playing a role of mediator. In this perspective, adult education plays a dual role. It can be a key element in the process of forced modernization of the most traditional roles, practices and cultures in society, and/or can be a model for the franchisement of disenfranchised populations, increasing social demand for good and services.

Literacy training becomes one of the central concerns as a means of social mobilization. The overall model of adult education is top-down, authoritarian, and compensatory, with the wishes and demands of communities channeled through patrimonial or corporatist structures of interest representation controlled by bureaucratic or technocratic institutions. Thus, adult education could play a subsidiary role of mass recruitment and training, challenging alternative and traditional channels of political participation such as political parties or trade unions. As such, adult education could eventually become part of a policy of political clientelism. The ideological foundation is the premise of technical progress through policy and planning with the expansion of massive systems of adult education, particularly in rural and underprivileged areas, with limited concern for quality of education provision. Thus as a perspective of political clientelism, any of the proposals for semi-autonomous participation of the communities (e.g. idealist pragmatism) or complete autonomy of communities (e.g. popular education) are rejected in the interest of corporatist channels of political representation.

The Transformative Power of Adult Learning Education

What is left if adult education has lost its transformative and empowering vision and mission, and why did this happen? The following sections will account for a number of reasons why adult education may have lost some of its power as a grand design and narrative of emancipation, emerging simply as part of an ever growing model of regulation in capitalist societies. However, despite this grim assessment, toward the end of this chapter, and particularly in Chapter Three, I will outline some new possibilities to reclaim the dream.

Adult education policy was not a priority for most governments in the twentieth century, and there is no reason to believe that this tendency will be drastically reversed in the twenty-first century, particularly when confronted by the globalization process and the requirements of a knowledge society (Desjardins, Rubenson, & Milana, 2006).

It has been documented by empirical research on adult education and lifelong learning policy that with exception of revolutionary processes, adult learning education as a policy area was not a governmental priority in the twentieth century (Arnove & Torres, 1996; Gadotti & Torres, 1994; Schugurensky & Torres, 1994; Torres, 1994, 1997; Torres & Schugurensky, 1996). There are numerous reasons for this.

First and principally, adult education serves a diverse clientele, yet a sizable majority of this clientele is a poor, politically under-represented, and consequently politically weak clientele, one usually limited in its ability to request, demand, and manipulate the social services of the State. Despite this overall assessment, it is clear that there are many "stakeholders" in adult learning education, and it cannot be restricted only to the powerless sectors in society.

Second, adult education institutions and programs are among the least prestigious in the hierarchy of formal and informal education. This is in part due to the nature of their clientele and, in part, because in the majority of cases, adult learning education programs do not offer prestigious academic credentials.

Third, connections between education and work are always elusive and consequently subject to multifarious theoretical debates, ideological confrontations, and political machinations. Despite the evident connection between apprenticeship programs and adult learning education, debates about the connection between adult education learning programs and the labor market are quite complex. Thus, discussions about the choices of investments in the area of education question the impact of adult professional training programs versus technical training at the job site. Many people argue that the investment in adult education has had limited impact as far as twentieth-century industrial production is concerned. The changes in the twenty-first century toward what is called a "knowledge-based" society may not be diminishing but rather enhancing this "policy gap" in adult education. This situation gives such questions particular relevance.

Fourth, policies having to do with adult education have always been implemented by the State in the area of social services. It follows that the State model and orientation bears directly on the conditions for investment and the expansion of policies in the area. The Nordic model of adult education, based on the notion of a welfare state model, seems to be one of the foremost successful experiences of adult learning education (Abrahamson, 2001; Antikainen, 2005, 2006; Antikainen, Harinen, & Torres, 2006; Kettunen, 2004; Torres & Antikainen, 2003).

Fifth, there are a variety of ideas and arguments that justify adult learning education policies, yet some of these ideas are contradictory. In Chapter One, I argued that as a field of inquiry, policy, research, and evaluation, adult learning education is under-theorized. In the next section, I offer six theoretical constructs aimed at explaining the theoretical and political rationale of the majority of the existing policies.

Despite the existence of a dominant idea among policymakers, there is no simple, non-contradictory, integrated idea that defends investments in specific programs. This should not be a surprise. Public sectors, and the technocratic as well as bureaucratic cadres that work in state institutions, tend to share a great deal of similarity in their rationale, policy operation, and the way they relate to program inputs and outputs. However, in the end, adult learning education, contrary to the majority of educational programs, is not a field easily manipulated and controlled by bureaucracies, technocracies or political cliques – though there are experiences to this extent. There is a community component in most adult education learning programs that makes them slightly different from other state-sponsored programs. Moreover, there are usually a number of social movements and NGOs linked to these programs, as was the case, for example, with the experiments undertaken worldwide in education for liberation, in popular education, and in the implementation of the educational philosophy advanced by Paulo Freire and people connected with this paradigm, or the myriad of educational experiences in nonformal education in Latin America today (O'Cadiz, Wong, & Torres, 1998).

Most social movements and some NGOs tend to be politically radical in their orientation and, as such, difficult for governmental institutions to control; adult learning education policies and programs, in cases like these, could threaten or be seen as threatening the status quo (Torres, 2011a, 2011b). The following section, drawing from the recent Latin American experience, shows some of the implications.

NEOLIBERALISM, THE NATION-STATE, AND SOCIAL MOVEMENTS: LESSONS FROM LATIN AMERICA[6]

"History is there, waiting for us to do something with it, waiting for us to confront immobilizing, neoliberal fatalism that maintains, for example, that the number of people unemployed in the world is a fin du siècle fatality... How is it possible for people in universities to claim that world unemployment is destiny? What did they read? How do they reason? No. In the world of culture, there is nothing fatalistically determined."

(Paulo Freire, The Gentle Scream)[7]

The past 25 years of Latin American education, culture, politics, and economics have seen the widespread implementation and failure of neoliberalism. This model of governance has been challenged in the past decade by the democratic election of social-democratic governments whose political platforms reject the basic rationale, policies, and programs of neoliberalism. Clear examples of these new policy narratives can be found in the platforms of Lula in Brazil, Néstor and Cristina Kirchner in Argentina, Hugo Chávez in Venezuela, José Mujica in Uruguay, and Evo Morales in Bolivia.

Despite its failures, however, neoliberalism has had considerable influence on educational research policy, planning, and evaluation agendas, not only in Latin America but also worldwide. For all practical purposes and measures, the No Child

Left Behind Act, the federal educational initiative of former U.S. President George W. Bush, is a child of neoliberalism (Olmos, Van Heertum, & Torres, 2010; Torres, 2009a; 2009b).

Neoliberalism has created "a new common sense" that has percolated into all public and private institutions and, by implication, into institutions of education, despite their apparent autonomy. Liberalism has been displaced by neoliberalism, deeply affecting education and social policies. As Michael W. Apple (2004) has argued:

> Liberalism itself is under concerted attack from the right, from the coalition of neo-conservatives, 'economic modernizers,' and new right groups who have sought to build a new consensus around their own principles. Following a strategy best called 'authoritarian populism,' this coalition has combined a 'free market ethic' with populist politics. The results have been a partial dismantling of social democratic policies that largely benefited working people, people of color, and women (these groups are obviously not mutually exclusive), the building of a closer relationship between government and the capitalist economy, and attempts to curtail liberties that had been gained in the past. (p. xxiv)

One may be tempted to argue that Latin America served as the experimental laboratory for the neoliberal educational agenda. Neoliberalism built a new common sense in education, leaving behind most of the established paradigms in the region, particularly the social democratic model that animated the educational outcomes of the New Deal, reflected in the perspectives of the "New School." This new common sense in education includes a strong drive towards privatization, decentralization, accountability, and testing, presenting an instrumental and economicist model of educational policy and planning based on the OECD's new conceptual hegemony – one that has updated and eventually surpassed the hegemony of the "banking model of education" of the World Bank. In adult education, this economicist perspective has been aptly criticized as "learning for earning" (Hake, 2006, p. 35; Lima, 2010).

Yet the OECD and World Bank promote an educational model that has an elective affinity with neoliberal top-down globalization models (Teodoro, 2009; Torres, 2010). There have been attempts to explain that there is a "common world educational culture" in the world system (Meyer, Kamens, & Benavot, 1992), but this new institutionalist approach fails to offer a precise political-economy analysis of what this commonality means. Because it lacks a political sociology of education approach, this neo-institutionalism also fails to show how the research, policy, and evaluation agenda of neoliberalism, dominant since the early eighties, has been formulated in the world system. Moreover, by failing to address the emergence of neoliberalism critically, this new institutionalist approach condones and perhaps even supports the overall tenets of the neoliberal agenda and its Western-centric capitalism perspective.

As an alternative model combining a political economy analysis with a political sociology of education, critical analyses focus on the Western-centric perspective emanating from the developments of economic neoliberalism, and its effects on education, reducing its role to service market liberalization and transforming the role of education for citizenship to education to serve a consumer (Robertson, 2003). This analysis suggests that there is a "globally structured educational agenda set by trans-national organizations" (Dale, 2000; Rizvi, 2006; Torres, 2009a).

Years ago, I argued that "defining the 'real' problems of education and the most appropriate (e.g. cost-effective, ethically acceptable, and legitimate) solutions depends greatly on the theories of the state that underpin, justify, and guide the educational diagnoses and the proposed solutions" (Torres, 1995b, p. 255). Thus, the transformation in the nature of the state (e.g. the emergence of the neoliberal state) and its implications for comparative analysis of adult education are very relevant. Otherwise we may not be able to understand the relationships between the state and public policy formation and the implications of adult education for development, particularly in the "conditioned states" located in the periphery of the capitalist world system (Arnove & Torres, 1995; Carnoy & Levin, 1985; Carnoy & Samoff, 1990; Torres, 1989, 1991b; Torres & Puiggrós, 1995; Torres & Schugurensky, 1994). Our empirical research with Daniel Schugurensky on adult education policy development in countries as diverse as Canada, Nicaragua, Mexico, and Tanzania shows the different and alternative rationales-in-use embedded in adult education policy formation (Schugurensky & Torres, 1994; Torres, 1996).

Since several national leaders in Latin America embraced the neoliberal model in the eighties and early nineties (for instance, Salinas de Gortari in Mexico, Carlos Saúl Menem in Argentina, and Fernando Henrique Cardoso in Brazil), and considering its effects on the subordinate social sectors in the region, particularly the increase in the region's inequality, neoliberalism has been deeply challenged by social movements, community organizations, and critical intellectuals. They have resisted the premises and policies of neoliberal governments and managed to support the emergence and growth of social democratic models of governance.

These "new" social movements differ greatly from the "old" social movements in the regions, however. First, they are territorially located and do not attempt to give regional or national answers to the social problems they confront. Second, they search for autonomy from governments and political parties. In this regard they consistently and continuously consult with the rank and file about their policies and actions. Third, instead of conceptually accepting the homogeneity of a national culture, they revalue the cultural identity of the social sectors that they represent. Fourth, they believe in their capacity to train their own organic intellectuals and educators — by implication, they do not trust schools and universities to help them organize. Fifth, there is a new and active leadership role for women – for instance, the highly visible female indigenous and *campesino* leadership exemplified by the Zapatista comandantes. Sixth, there is a constant preoccupation with the organization of labor and the question of sustainable development in the process of production. Consequently they strive for new forms of hierarchy and equity pay in the process of work and for organizational forms of production that will not damage the environment. And last but not least, they promote new forms of instrumental action to carry out their demands. While the old social movements' favorite weapon was the labor strike, the new social movements occupy spaces, streets, plazas, and squares (like the mothers of the Plaza de Mayo) and even cities (e.g. the Cordobazo in the early sixties) (Zibecchi, 2003, n/d).

These new movements create a visible and prominent presence in urban environments, placing their membership at odds with the majority of the urban middle classes. The action of the *piqueteros* in Buenos Aires is a prime example of this growing conflict between the subordinate social sectors and the middle classes. Finally, they have helped unleash a new era, one that analysts such as Marco Aurelio García, Lula's principal advisor on international relations, call "post-neoliberalism" as the strategy to overcome global crises.[8]

ADULT LEARNING EDUCATION: MODELS AND RATIONALITIES AS THEORETICAL CONSTRUCTS

"The materialist doctrine concerning the changing of circumstances and upbringing forgets that circumstances are changed by men and that it is essential to educate the educator himself."

Karl Marx, *III Thesis on Feurbach*[9]

It is possible to analyze the roles and purposes of adult learning education policy by discussing six rationales for policymaking. These rationales, when transformed into policy, may take the form of constitutional mandates, investment in human capital, political socialization, compensatory legitimation, international pressures, and social movements. These rationales are analyzed later in Chapter Three, but it is important to first highlight some of the key elements of the hegemonic narratives in adult learning education.

Despite the rhetoric underlying a particular policy narrative, the dominant logic among policymakers in adult education is instrumental rationality, and technocratic thinking is the dominant *weltanschauung* in adult education policy planning. Discussing the notion of instrumental rationality as developed by Weber (the rule of impersonal economic forces and bureaucratic administration), it is possible to document how the ideology of the welfare state has resulted in a de-politicization of policymakers' view regarding the social world.

In my recent thesis on neoliberalism's new common sense (Torres, 2011b) I argue that neoliberalism has utterly failed as a viable model of economic development, yet the politics of culture associated with neoliberalism is still in force and has become the new common sense shaping the role of government and education. This "common sense" has become an ideology playing a major role in constructing hegemony as moral and intellectual leadership in contemporary societies.

Here is the political paradox that neoliberalism has brought to the fore: while the discourse is depoliticizing, the narrative predicated by neoliberalism re-politicizes educational environments, agendas, and policies toward models of regulations inside educational fields – contrary to the attempt to deregulate state fiscal and financial policies – and against emancipatory practices. Let us go back for a minute to the contributions of German social scientist and philosopher Jürgen Habermas. For Habermas the pursuit of knowledge in the human sciences can be better understood as guided by three fundamental knowledge-guiding interests rather than by a single explanatory factor. There is an empirical-analytical knowledge, but there are also historical-hermeneutic interests and critical emancipatory knowledge. Similarly, cognitive-instrumental rationality can be differentiated from moral-practical rationality and from aesthetic-practical rationality.

While the notion of power is clearly expressed in the narratives of education policymakers, they have no conceptual expressions of emancipatory action or heuristic analyses of social action. Let us take policy language as an example. The language of policymakers tends to be technically aseptic and non-controversial, borrowing conceptual categories from system theories, human capital, and functionalist or neo-functionalist paradigms, and more recently and increasingly from the world of business. The impact on education has been felt at several levels, but none as relevant as the presence of a "culture of science" in the politics of inquiry. It has been argued that:

> The entire discourse on education science reflects a number of distinct, but mutually constitutive, political forces or movements using science to shape what we can think, and thus, what we can become in the so-called postmodern age. These forces or movements are, briefly (1) the movement to professionalize educational researchers, (2) the attempts to restrict democracy via scientism, (3) the uses of academic classification for organizing the world into social groups, (4) the imperatives of the informational society, which seek precision in order to convert the world into 'data' for governing, and (5) the effects of transnational capitalist exchanges, which convert everything into a cost-benefit analysis and make us all complicit in ways we do not fully grasp. (Baez & Boyles, 2009, p. vii)

While policymakers and policy planners may pay lip service to some of the determinants of social action and use this "culture of science" to legitimate policy and planning, in the end, key dimensions in policy formation, such as social class differences, gender, ethnic or racial discrimination, or discrimination based on region of origin, immigration status, or religion remains understated in the narratives of policymakers. This is so because, as it is known in theories of organization, the sharper the conceptual categorization of a phenomenon, the more difficult it becomes to set policy that will accommodate multiple interests and incompatible goals within any organization.

Models and Rationalities of Adult Learning Education

Three models seem to prevail in adult learning education propelled by state institutions. These are a "therapeutic model", a "recruitment or franchisement model," and a "forced modernization model." There is a fourth model, which for the sake of brevity I will name a "revolutionary model." However, by virtue of their own inception and dynamics, and the patterns of social and political control of the world system, revolutionary models tend to be short-lived and hence transitional. A fifth model, still in its infancy, could emerge if policy and practice are politically oriented toward social emancipatory transformation and not simply regulation. This model could be named a social compact in adult learning education between state institutions and social movements. For the moment, I will analyze the dominant models that have been in place for more than three decades – whether or not they have been recognized by policymakers and state institutions – and will start addressing briefly the fourth transitional model of revolution. At the end of this section, I will highlight some of the possible orientations in a new social compact in adult learning education.

The revolutionary model while in its inception will have a very different orientation from that of the former models, constituting in essence a transitional model that, as history has shown, may evolve toward one of the three existing models. While it does not necessarily have to be this way, and models of empowerment do not have to evolve toward either of the three "normal" models of ALE, empirical data shows that more often than not, revolutionary models are short-lived, transitional, perhaps even ephemeral, and that the routinization of the revolutionary charisma will eventually evolve into one the models listed above. Yet their cathartic nature and the revolutionary mystique and lessons that emerged in and substantiate the revolutionary process will endure longer than the historical experience per se, and as such these values and mystique embody the notion of education as the possible dream, and hence the motto of the World Social Forum that "another world is possible" (Torres & Noguera, 2008). Revolutionary models of adult education, what Paulo Freire termed "Cultural Action for Freedom" (Freire, 1972, 1973), are both utopian and utopistic:

> Utopia is a term used here in the sense of philosopher Paul Ricoeur, as ucronia, that is, the symbolic representation of a time reconfigured by narrative fiction. In the realm of social sciences, Immanuel Wallerstein has resorted to a term he coined, utopistics, as a way to evaluate the historical choices of the twenty-first century. (Torres & Teodoro, 2007, pp. 1–8)

Thus, there is a role in social sciences in evaluating through utopistics the "historical choices" of the new century, as Wallerstein puts it, and there always will be utopian models that will capture the imagination of the people and new collective action alternatives to bureaucratic rationalization and instrumental knowledge.

But let us go back to the argument of the main models of ALE and their differences. Analytical and empirical research shows that in "therapeutic models" the state appears as a benefactor, and the problems of poverty, illiteracy, and adult learning education are seen either as the result of temporary economic dislocations that may be adjusted through market mechanisms or as the result of individual deficits in skills or attitudes, which may be addressed through instructional means. The role of the experts is to determine the nature of the training given to the individuals, who should be integrated into the job market as soon as possible. Teachers are treated as professionals who used to enjoy great autonomy that is now clearly diminishing.

In the "recruitment or franchisement model," emphasis is placed on a constant and active attraction of large numbers of learners to adult education programs. The rationale seems to be the incorporation of a disenfranchised clientele into the dominant political model. Teachers are mainly volunteers and follow textbooks designed by central government agencies or international agencies. In this model, the main concern is not the quality of learning, but the recruitment and massive control of large numbers of people who otherwise could remain outside the corporatist channels of political participation.

Finally, in "forced modernization" models, the emphasis is placed on capital accumulation through the implementation of modern agricultural techniques and increasing the country's integration into the world economy. Such a model is generally resisted both by women, who produce for home consumption, and by young males, whose main interest in attending adult learning education programs is to gain employment in urban areas, thus leaving the rural enclaves.

The three models share common traits that are surprising considering the diversity of living conditions, state structures, and political philosophies in which they take place. By and large, all three models are non-participative, where social and political issues, as well as issues that may bring conflict into the operation of adult learning education services, are ignored or perceived exclusively as problems that can be fixed through technical measures. This is the fundamental difference with a "revolutionary model," which, in its inception and narratives is based in the active participation and political organization of diverse sectors within civil society and the political society.

Second, in most societies, and at best if enough attention is paid, adult education is a clear instrument of the state contributing to capital accumulation and political legitimation practices, neglecting any emancipatory practices that may empower learners or communities. Once again, particularly at the beginning of the establishment of "revolutionary models," adult education is conceived as an instrument of the state for the political organization of groups, mostly through class-based emancipatory narratives.

Third, in all three models, literacy training is either irrelevant or marginal, isolated from productive work and skill upgrading programs. By contrast, literacy training campaigns, such as in the socialist experiences of Cuba, Nicaragua or Grenada, are crucial for the organization of "revolutionary models" of adult education, mostly inspired in the paradigm of popular education (Arnove, 1986; Arnove & Torres, 1995; Torres, 1990b, 1995b).

Fourth, in the absence of participatory organizational structures and practices, a top-down decision-making system prevails. Despite the operation of three different models of adult education oriented by divergent political and philosophical values, all offer few opportunities for the learners or community to participate in policymaking.

Fifth, teachers rarely have any training in adult education, and the same can be said about the glaring lack of specialists in adult learning education research, policy, and evaluation. In developed market democracies, highly professional teachers trained to work with children and youth often have a patronizing and paternalistic attitude regarding adult learners. In developing countries, paraprofessional and poorly trained teachers present high rates of job turnover and absenteeism, which in turn lead to high student dropout rates.

Lastly, there is evidence that almost everywhere adult learning education programs are organized in a two-track system: a more prestigious one focused on programs for upgrading skills for the inception in the world of labor, and a marginal one that emphasizes adult basic education and literacy training (Torres, 1991a, 1996; Torres & Schugurensky, 1994).

There are other alternatives, and the one that I see as very promising is a model of development based on a new social compact among the state, social movements, and civil society. Table 2 offers some comparative arguments.

Based on social contract theory, a new social compact seeks to link individuals and organizations such as NGOs and social movements with the broader segments of civil society, attempting to articulate a new social compact that redirects political energies and financial resources to reinforce new models of adult learning education. Most social contract arguments underscore that individuals (and in this case I should also argue, institutions) consent either implicitly or explicitly to surrender some of their freedoms submitting to some authority (in democracies, the rule of the majority) in order to gain through organized governance the protection of the legal rights that have not been surrendered. This implies that the new social compact will protect the collective legal rights while at the same time seeking new models of political participation and political deliberation as the basis for social contract theory, linking adult learning literacy with the broader goals of the knowledge society, and also making this construct an attempt to democratize the culture and knowledge per se. There are many small experiments worldwide in which this new social compact could be based, but so far I have not observed a larger coalition trying to integrate this new model, beyond the installation of a revolutionary model, in the realm of society. However, the challenge of scale, with the appropriate political will, can be overcome.

Table 2. State rationality and ALE models

Categories for analysis: Goals and Principles	Welfare State Model[1]	Recruitment Franchisement model[2]	Forced Modernization Model[3]	Revolutionary (a transitional model)	Popular Public ALE/ Partnerships and alliances
Rationale	Therapeutic Model. State as a Benefactor Instrumental rationality	Political Mobilization Model. Goal is to franchise disenfranchised populations Instrumental rationality	Modernization of agrarian regions via extensionism and literacy Instrumental rationality	Mobilization of population for revolutionary purposes New models of community organizations in partnership with state institutions Revolutionary mystique Instrumental rationality mixed with emancipatory rationality	Participatory budgeting, participatory planning, participatory partnerships to deal with micro and macro crises, and collaboration between a democratic state and popular organizations from civil society Communicative Rationality (including cognitive instrumental, moral-practical and aesthetic practical rationalities)
Participatory/ non-participatory	Top-Down Decision-making Compensatory legitimation	Top-Down Decision Making Compensatory legitimation	Top-Down Decision Making Authoritarian legitimation	Top-Down Decision Making with high mobilization Revolutionary legitimation	Participatory based on a social compact between government and civil society organizations

Narrative	Individual deficit or temporary economic dislocation	Incorporation in the model of political development, controlled political participation	Education for development in rural areas	Cultural Action for Freedom Empowerment of subordinate populations, Elimination of the "Culture of Silence"	ALE as a human right. A culture of alliances and negotiations in equal standing, with renewed state funding to ALE. Alliances for empowerment of people's identities.
ALE orientation	Compensatory	Compensatory	Compensatory	Compensatory /Redistributionist	Redistributionist, pursuing models of empowerment and collaboration in human rights and sustainable development
Main problem to be solved	Deficits (individual and social) to be solved through welfare measures	Lack of Participation and representation Deficits (individual and social).	Lack of productivity in the rural areas, and lack of social organization and services	Creation of a Militant mentality, incentivation of a revolutionary mystique, organization of the People's organizations through State's control	Multidimensional deliberation and participation of institutions from civil society and several institutions of the democratic states (different Ministries and Secretaries) engaged in partnerships

(Continued)

31

Table 2. Continued

Categories for analysis: Goals and Principles	Welfare State Model[1]	Recruitment Franchisement model[2]	Forced Modernization Model[3]	Revolutionary (a transitional model)	Popular Public ALE/ Partnerships and alliances
Teachers and/or ALE facilitators or coordinators	Professionals but mostly trained in schooling models for children	Voluntaries or Facilitators with limited training	Voluntaries or Facilitators with limited training	Voluntaries or Facilitators with limited training but highly active in social movements and grass-roots organizations	Voluntaries and/or professional teachers but educated in a culture of collaboration, dialogue, and lifelong education with a strong constructivist perspective.

[1] To be sure, there are diverse types of governmental welfare regime. Several classifications draw upon the influential work of Danish scholar Gøsta Esping-Andersen, who distinguished between social-democratic welfare regimes (e.g. Sweden and the Nordic countries), liberal welfare regimes (like the USA) and conservative welfare regimes (such as Germany). There is a modification of this typology developed by Walther et all, distinguishing four types: universalistic (Nordic), employment-centered (Netherlands, France, Germany), liberal (Ireland, U.K., USA), and sub-protective welfare regimes (Italy, Spain and Portugal). Gøsta Esping-Andersen, *The Three Worlds of Welfare Capitalism.* Cambridge, Cambridge University Press, 1990; Andreas Walther, "Regimes of Youth Transitions. Choice, Flexibility and Security in Young People's Experiences across Different European Contexts." Young: *Nordic Journal of Youth Research,* 14 (2), 2006: 119–139.

[2] The government regimes grouped under this label are usually termed corporatist and/or populist, and have predominated in a number of low income, developing countries, and in some emergent countries. To be sure, there are even differences in the way these forms of governance are described, but in general, they include models of negotiations of diverse corporations (e.g. unions, management) mediated by state intervention in decision making. This view of corporatism tends to emphasize the presence of corporatist ideologies in the bosom of the civil society, and hence there is some elective affinity of civil society with state governance models. The second, more restrictive view of corporatism, stresses centralized forms of negotiations in the constitution of a social compact. For a description of both types of government regimes, in ideal form, see for instance, Guillermo O'Donnell, Philippe C. Schmitter, and Laurence Whitehead, *Transitions from Authoritarian Rule: Latin America.* Baltimore, Maryland, Johns Hopkins University Press, 1993.

[3] Developmental regimes grouped under this category may encompass a vast array of models, from typical dictatorships, to low income, developing societies with limited democratic governance, or outright 'authoritarian' models based on 'caudillos' or a strong executive that controls the juridical and the parliamentary system. They usually include societies with a large agrarian base.

NOTES

1   http://www.kenwilber.com/home/landing/index.html
2   See for instance, *Creating a New Paradigm for Business* by John Mackey, CEO, Whole Foods Market co-founder, FLOW.
3   See for instance, Lohas, *Lifetime of Health and Sustainability* [www.lohas.com].
4   Freire, P. "Pedagogy of the City." Cited in Carlos Alberto Torres, *Democracy, Education and Multiculturalism*. Op. Cit, p. 161.
5   See the resource library for popular education and community participation at http://www.popednews.org/collection/poped_titles.htm
6   Excerpts from Torres, 2011, reproduced with authorization of the International Review of Education.
7   Op. cit., p. 70.
8   Dialogo. Reportaje a Carlos Piñeiro Iñiguez, *Página 12*, Monday, July 12, 2010, p. 12. http://www.pagina12.com.ar/diario/dialogos/21-149326-2010-07-12.html
9   http://www.marxists.org/archive/marx/works/1845/theses/theses.htm, retrieved June 2, 2011.

CHAPTER III

RATIONALITIES IN ADULT LEARNING EDUCATION

Six rationalities seem to provide the explanation for the nuanced texture and dynamics of adult learning education policies. They are: a) constitutional mandates; b) human capital investment; c) political socialization; d) compensatory legitimization; e) international pressures; and f) social movements.

Constitutional Mandates

A legalistic perspective would be based on constitutional recommendations or mandates to the effect that it is the right of every citizen to be literate and educated, thus having access to adult learning education. Non-literate citizens, or those who have not completed primary school or secondary education, or who need to be retraining and "retooled" to catch up with the world of work, should have the opportunity to do so.

The argument has the following logic:

1. On the one hand, adult learning education is a fundamental instrument in the consolidation of citizenship (as opposed to the constitution of an elite);
2. On the other hand, basic education is a substantial source of the general welfare of all citizens;
3. Finally, adult education should be provided by the State as one of its policies of assistance or welfare. Such policies aid the consolidation of democracy as a system of political participation and representation. However we should be careful here, because the concept of democracy is a sliding signifier, meaning different things to different people. Democracy (as civic and political democracy) is usually conceived as a mode of decision-making assuming collectively binding rules and policies over which the people exercise control. Hence the most democratic arrangement exists when all members of the collectivity enjoy effective equal rights to directly take part in the decision-making process (Beetham, 1993, p. 55). There is no doubt that legal arguments can be criticized for being overly formal and apolitical when it comes to identifying the motivation behind such policies and, what is more, they fail to guarantee the application of these policies – in other words, there is always some distance between legal norms and real practice.

Human Capital Investment

Adult learning education as an investment in human capital offers an economist's vision. In this vision, it is argued that adult learning education, and particularly literacy, extensionism, and work apprenticeship programs, stimulate economic development in different ways:

a. It increases the productivity of people who have recently become literate and/or educated through different modalities and programs of adult learning education;
b. It increases the productivity of people who work with the recently ALE educated;
c. It expands the diffusion of generalized knowledge for the individual (important in terms of health), reducing the cost of transmitting useful knowledge. In Europe, it is common to try to make indexes of lifelong learning (see OECD, *Social Outcomes of Learning*) and to assume that learning has direct effects on health and welfare. Without sufficient empirical documentation, this assumption or hypothesis looks exaggerated, missing some of the theoretical suggestions and critiques from reproduction theories;
d. It stimulates the demand for technical and vocational training;
e. It functions as an instrument of selection for more able workers, broadening their occupational mobility and emphasizing economic incentives, in other words, reinforcing the tendency of people to respond positively to a pay raise based on personal effort;
f. Finally, it creates conditions for people who have fallen out of the schooling pipeline to return to a formal and nonformal educational pipeline, linking them with the demands of the labor markets, and in an optimal societal situation, facilitating their inception in global economic dynamics.

The economic argument can be criticized on several aspects. First, the economic benefits of literacy training and of adult basic education, particularly in developing countries, are not properly documented by empirical research. For instance, there are some schools of thought that claim that literacy is more important from a cultural standpoint than an economic one.

Second, there is the problem of what might be called "the diploma disease." Considering the excessive number of credentials in modern capitalist societies, courses concluded without being able to guarantee salary increases become less appealing to workers. In this context, employers may begin to create new selection criteria that lead, in turn, to an increase in the number of credentials. At the same time, once they have reached a certain level of educational experience and training, many workers find themselves priced out of labor markets.

Finally, neoclassic arguments about how it makes sense to have homogeneous markets notwithstanding, the majority of labor markets are segmented rather than homogeneous. Markets that might be affected by adult learning education tend not to facilitate stability since their social benefits are scarce or non-existent and the available workforce is largely unqualified. These facts make training programs for adults seemingly less attractive in terms of economic returns unless they are intimately related to apprenticeship policies at the state level, and particularly if they are intimately related to the training policies of trade unions. The European experience of the past fifteen years and the new dynamics of apprenticeship training certification exemplify this fact. Consequently, there is a growing disparity between the mechanisms of employability and the levels of qualification offered by adult education programs.

Political Socialization

Training in citizenship is often considered a central point in the socialization process of adult education. Adult learning education of captive populations, for instance people in correctional centers, raises the question of how adult learning education can be used for improving the life chances of people incarcerated, while at the same time, raising their consciousness. People who are just learning to read, to write, and to use basic mathematics, or who have developed marginal levels of adult learning education remain limited and marginal "enlightened" citizens. In this way, reading and writing become prerequisites for the exercise of the basic rights of citizenship and, occasionally, a source of rebellion or revolt (Creppell, 1989; Markoff, 1986).

However, confident belief that more education for adults will result in their making better use of citizenship does not ameliorate the following scenarios. Citizenship could be manipulated by a series of educational activities that are nothing less than indoctrination.[1] The reverse is also possible: Adult learning education programs could promote postures of resistance to the basic organizing principles of the political status quo, as was the case in many educational programs aimed at the working classes and organized during the twentieth century, or as is the case with several perspectives of religious education for adults inspired in fundamentalist religious traditions such as the Islamic Brotherhood in Egypt, a parallel form of indoctrination as some of the madrassas are for young people. On the other hand, the idea of promoting education for citizenship is sometimes based on the idea of a shared consensus, something that has proven to be highly questionable in contemporary societies facing the crisis of legitimacy of the State, and the crisis of political representation in what is known as the ingovernability of democracies.

Compensatory Legitimation

In a different scenario, adult learning education may be seen as a way for the government to gain legitimacy, in the context of increasingly ungovernable and pluralistic societies. In this sense, adult learning education could be considered an instrument for the promotion of symbolic participation in the political system. In other words, as part of a strategy of compensatory legitimation including leveraging academic experience for the planning, participation, and support of the judicial system (legalization of educational politics) in the constitution of a social order affected by a crisis of legitimacy (Weiler, 1983, pp. 259–277).

I have argued for the past three decades that adult education policy is usually oriented to prepare people for secondary labor markets, where job stability is limited, income low and fragmented, social benefits scarce or nonexistent, and the supply of low skilled labor abundant. Likewise, I have shown that adult education has been usually co-opted by the State and employed as an instrument of social legitimation and the extension of state authority, more than as a tool for self-reliance of individuals and communities, not only in the poor segments of Latin American and Third World societies, but also in industrial advanced capitalist societies (Torres, 1989, 1996; Torres, Pannu, & Bacchus, 1993).

International Pressures

Moreover, adult learning education politics can be seen as a response on the part of the State to the pressures of the international system. For example, the indicators of international prestige consider levels of development and of literacy crucial. In the same way, progress in women's education advocated by many international organizations, including the World Bank, is seen as an indicator of more balanced distribution of resource and societal equality. The launching of Education For All in 1990 and the roles assigned to adult education have been instrumental in rousing governments to reactivate adult learning education models and institutions.

In this way, a reawakened interest in literacy on the part of many societies in the last century became a way to avoid international embarrassment. The role of UNESCO in promoting adult learning education has been central since its creation, as has been the notion of human rights, promoted by the United Nations system, which is creating a global political system, impinging upon the constitutional prescriptions and operations of most of the world's nations. We will come back to discuss the dilemmas of human rights for adult learning education in Chapter Four.

Social Movements

Finally, adult education can be seen as part of a new social movement, or could be effectively used by social movements in their quest for policy leverage. Few adult learning education programs have contributed to human liberation or served as mechanisms of social and political participation. Few have tried to put education and knowledge at the service of the least favored social strata. Fewer still have attempted to experiment by making adult education an initial stimulus to more encompassing social movements (Chrabolowsky, 2003; Gohn, 2008), yet some have developed trends toward increasing the autonomy of adults. Adult education as a pedagogy of opposition is an honored tradition in radical education, and the paradigm of popular education emerges as an emblematic tradition (Crowther, Johnston, Martin, & Merrill, 2006; Huttunen & Suoranta, 2006; Mayo, 2007).

If we understand politics as a struggle for power, new social movements should not be interpreted exclusively in political terms, as they also represent cultural and moral practices centered on the construction of collective identities and spaces. They originate around certain demands and specific social relations, becoming increasingly autonomous for traditional institutions of political representation of interest. This is because, as proponents of social movement theory, individuals no longer exclusively define their identity only in relation to the means and relations of production but also as consumers, residents of a particular neighborhood, members of churches, ethnic or gender groups, and participants in the political system. A distinctive characteristic of new social movements is their cognitive and ideological focus on rethinking preexisting social and cultural paradigms as part of a politics of identity (Torres, 1998b, pp. 421–447).

A pedagogy of opposition is intimately related to cultures of activism:

> Cultures of activism…are collective expressions of oppositional behavior, thought, symbols, and action that arise as groups of individuals seek societal or institutional change in specific settings…[they] may be connected to larger social struggles but are not synonymous with them. (Saltzman, 2001, p. 194)

Instrumental Rationality and Policymaking

While all these rationales may be present in the policy orientation, the dominant ideology among policymakers, particularly in advanced industrial capitalism, seems to be based on technocratic thinking oriented by a mixture of populist traditions and conservative politics. By and large, adult learning education policies have been guided by models of instrumental rationality.

Instrumental rationality is governed by technical rules based on empirical knowledge and suggests the ability to forecast events likely to produce action. In other words, it is governed by technical rules seeking precise control of social and physical events. Thus, instrumental rationality involves a substantive purpose of domination—although one exercised as German philosopher Herbert Marcuse has suggested through methodological and scientific calculations and control.

There are still numerous questions about the future of adult education as instrumental rationality in the globalization process. Will globalization open a window for alternative rationalities in adult education? I will turn now to a discussion of how globalization intertwines with collective opposition and the implications for adult learning education.

NEOLIBERAL GLOBALIZATION AND COLLECTIVE OPPOSITION: POTENTIAL IMPACTS ON ADULT LEARNING EDUCATION

In Chapter Two, I discussed globalization processes as a key concept in the analysis. Yet it is imperative to situate the global, national, and regional reality of adult learning education in the context of a global economy, which operates in very different ways from the former twentieth century industrial economy.

This new global economy, characterized as Toyotism, is more fluid and flexible, with multiple layers of power and decision-making. The old economy, characterized as Fordism, was based on high volume and highly standardized production with a few managers controlling the production process from above and a great number of workers following orders. This economy of mass production was stable as long as it could reduce costs of production, including the price of labor, and retool quickly enough to stay competitive. Because of advancements in transportation and communications technology and the growth of the service industry, production has become fragmented around the world. Mobile capital allows production to move to locations where there is either cheaper or more highly trained labor, favorable political conditions, along with access to better infrastructure and national resources, larger markets and/or tax incentives. While the public education system and adult learning education in the old Fordist capitalist order was oriented toward the production of a disciplined and reliable workforce, the new global economy seems to have redefined labor relations, challenging our perception of the role of education in development.

How do these transformations in the world economy specifically affect education around the world, particularly in developing countries? The oil and debt crisis of the 1970s and the early 1980s spurred the introduction of structural adjustment policies under IMF and World Bank supervision, intended to "fix" ailing economies. Structural adjustment policies require financial and public sector restructuring to stabilize economies and sustain economic growth. They are based on principles of free trade, reduction of public expenditures, and privatization. Thus neoliberalism has been intertwined with the new phenomena that have been termed globalization (Torres, 2009a, 2009b).

There are many definitions of globalization, or perhaps more accurately, there are many globalizations. For example, globalization has been defined by British political scientist David Held, following Sir Anthony Giddens, as the intensification of worldwide social relations which link distant localities in such a way that local happenings are shaped by events occurring many miles away and vice versa. Another view presented in the work of Australian social scientists Allan and Carmen Luke sees globalization as a feature of late capitalism, or the condition of postmodernity, and, more importantly, as the emergence of a world system driven in large part by a global capitalist economy. Urry see globalization as the transformation of time and space in which complex interactions and exchanges once impossible become everyday activities. Still influential sociologists like Manuel Castells and Alain Touraine see globalization as an assault on traditional notions of society and the nation-state whereby the very nature of citizenship and social change is dramatically altered.

For the purposes of this chapter, "globalization may be defined quite simply as increasing global interconnectedness, a number of complex and interlinked processes are theorized under the heading of 'globalization,' principally economic, technological, cultural, environmental, and political processes. Globalization involves flows of goods, capital, people, information, ideas, images, and risks across national borders, combined with the emergence of social networks and political institutions which constrain the nation-state" (Nash, 2000, p. 47).

Not surprisingly, top-down neoliberal models of globalization have encountered fierce opposition from several social actors, and the recent financial crises have unveiled the end of the neoliberal era. The predominance of neoliberalism with its policies of less regulation, more privatization, and diminishing roles for the nation-states is over. It will be replaced, though the format, structures, and dynamics of the new world system are still unclear. However what does seem to be clear is that the new model of economic development will be state-centered. With the rescue packaged proposed by the defenders of ultra-capitalism – or what some have termed "market fundamentalism" such as the Bush administration – passed by the U.S. Congress in October 2008, it seems that even the most recalcitrant market fundamentalists have succumbed to the realities of the dramatic failure of neoliberalism. That is the dramatic failure of checks and balances in the financial system, increased levels of international indebtedness, extreme market volatility, and fiscal deficit in the larger economy of the world, which is dragging the rest of the advanced capitalist countries, along with many of the emerging countries, into what seems a financial abyss. This phenomenon seems to have affected, with various degrees of impact, most economies – perhaps with the qualified exception of a few Asian economies, which have enough equity to ride the web of defaults.

The international anti-globalization and social justice/equality movements seem to bring together active spirits, among whom important voices of dissent are beginning to appear. The cast of characters includes "strange bedfellows," from the late Pope John Paul II, who before the 2002 meeting of the G-7 countries asked that the debts of the Third World countries be pardoned and beseeched the leaders of wealthy nations to pay more attention to the problem of poverty in this neoliberal age, to the well-known French sociologist, Pierre Bourdieu, an esteemed professor at the Collège de France, who guided educators at the beginning of the 1970s with his work on education as social reproduction. Bourdieu, in a pessimistic tone, compared globalization and neoliberalism to the most infamous disease of the twentieth century: AIDS. Unwavering in his position in respect to the G-8 nations meeting in Genoa, Bourdieu claimed that "the violence of the masses is useful in one way at least: it forces the leading actors of neoliberalism who like to appear calm, serene and rational, to demonstrate their own violence" (Bourdieu, 2001, p. 18).

The end of the Cold War witnessed the transformation of the world into a new global economy, characterized by rapid technological advances, with increasingly agile financial transactions in deregulated capital markets. Job mobility also increased, justifying the thoughts of a Los Angeles journalist who wrote, "borders are convenient political lines – lines that are crossed if history demonstrates that it is necessary" (Martinez, 2001, p. 2).

The Genoa debacle revealed new political and intellectual realities to the globalizing world. On the one hand, it proved that a multinational social movement of disparate allies, including factions of the Roman Catholic and Protestant churches, Greenpeace, groups defending the rights of local communities and the rights of feminists, and a panoply of anarchist and socialist movements from advanced countries were not afraid to confront the chiefs of State of the eight most industrialized nations on the planet. Russian representatives also attended, invited at the last minute for political motives rather than as the emissaries of an industrial power comparable to the rest. On the other hand, it also showed that when these leaders are confronted by anti-globalization movements, they have less control than they do over the world economy – this has been evidenced by the recent debacle of the financial markets, and the inability of the IMF to predict the crisis, let alone to suggest a viable technical and political avenue for solutions. It is this fact that has led some analysts to argue that we are witnessing a corporate take-over of the world rather than its globalization. Similarly, Brazilian sociologist Octavio Ianni was struck by the notion of the difference between globalization as an ineluctable historical process, and globalism, as a process articulated by neoliberalism and coordinated by global corporations (Ianni, 1993, 1996; Romão, 2001).

The European Union is an example of national borders supplanted by economic realpolitik. Postmodern mass media cultures are coming face-to-face with local communities and traditional cultures, and new movements founded in cosmopolitan democracies and based on human rights programs are being confronted by fresh outbreaks of ethnic nationalism. What is more, business analysts like Kenichi Ohmae have denounced the nation-state as something from the past, arguing that the main creators of wealth are being constructed in regional states (Ohmae, 1995).

From his neoliberal perspective, Ohmae adds to his devastating criticism of the nation-state a critique of liberal democracies, the targets of growing popular demand for minimal public services that they are no longer able to satisfy (Ohmae, 1990, 1995). Ohmae's argument might be considered a right-wing version of what O'Connor calls the "fiscal crisis of the State" (O'Connor, 1973) and Habermas sees as a "dilemma of legitimation" (Habermas, 1975).

It has become a moot point to argue the relevance of such questions for adult learning education since "particularly during the twentieth century, educational systems and practices were maintained, prepared, organized and certified by the State. In fact, public education is a State function not only in terms of legal order or of financial support. The specific requirements for certification, the requirements and basic qualifications of teachers, the definition of textbooks, and obligatory courses in the basic curriculum are controlled by official agencies and defined by specific State policies" (Torres, 1998a, p. 14).

In the neoliberal model of globalization, educational policies are internationally promoted according to agendas defined by multinational and bilateral organizations like the World Bank, the IMF, OECD, or the IDB (Interamerican Development Bank), as well as some agencies of the United Nations. Such agendas include a tendency to favor the privatization and decentralization of public education as part of an attempt to deregulate State activities and, eventually, to "downsize" government, allied to a movement to standardize academic performance, as defined by tests. This movement wants to regulate the way schools function, as well as teacher training and academic achievement, particularly insofar as they influence the performance level of higher education.

Globalizations are having an impact on educational politics throughout the world and, thus, it comes as no surprise that such a movement is also affecting the politics of adult learning education.

ADULT LEARNING EDUCATION: WHAT IS TO BE DONE?

This brief theoretical review has identified several models and rationalities of adult learning education, and contextualized them in view of the dynamics of globalization processes affecting the world system. Adult learning education as compensatory legitimation, as a legalistic perspective, and/or as training for citizenship and socialization may have lost relevance in terms of policy rationality in neolliberal times. Yet recent crises may propel it to a position of prominence in the reconstruction of the world system. Changes in social policies and public restructuring point to less investment in the political legitimacy of the State which, in turn, has resulted in a process of privatization of public services under neoliberalism; though that phenomenon seems to have quickly reverted with new social arrangements that are state-centred.

It has been some time since adult education was abandoned by the State as training for the traditional (industrial) workforce. Perhaps with the honorable exception of apprenticeship programs in the European Union, many on-the-job training and training-for-jobs programs remain in the hands of the business community or duly supported by trade unions rather than state institutions — apprenticeship programs in the United States have systematically declined in the past three decades. Technological advances with powerful implications are diminishing the number of well-paid and qualified jobs as well as the level of trade unionism (which usually applies pressure for more worker training), and reinforcing the tendency for employment in the service sector, which will drastically change the model of adult learning education proclaimed by the "old economy," based on technical and jobsite training. The growing outsourcing of jobs makes this scenario all the more complicated.

Despite the new avenues opened up by the creation of new post-neoliberal arrangements,[2] adult learning education will continue to jockey for space with new social movements that are being inserted in the globalization process. Eventually, the adult education policies (like those practiced in the city of Porto Alegre, in the south of Brazil) or informal programs (like people's libraries for the unemployed in Argentina), or the projects based on the Sarvodaya Shramadana Movement in India, are part and parcel of emerging social movements of protest, opposition, and resistance, like those involved in the confrontation in Genoa and in many places before and after the Genoa experience.[3] This process will reinforce the tradition of adult education as a tool for the political organization of disadvantaged populations, a notion well represented in the field of popular education.

Even the dominant logic coming from the standpoint of technocratic thinking and influenced by a mixture of populist traditions and conservative politics in the area of adult education will not be adequate in the context of globalization. This fact will be of greater consequence in countries of the Third World where the latest wave of poverty and social inequity has swollen to tsunami proportions.

On the level of compensatory politics, investment options recommend a flow of direct aid to oppressed populations affected by economic restructuring, unemployment, and poverty. As far as educational measures are concerned, particularly in the poorer countries, basic and elementary education for children continues to dominate the attention of policymakers who will continue to demand as much attention as they did in the twentieth century, reducing the chance of any initiative in the area of adult learning education.

Finally, the implications of the "knowledge society" for adult education are still unclear, and more empirical research is needed. In the meantime, if we may risk an opinion: the economicist argument that we need to train adults for the job market is not going to be as convincing in the context of the "knowledge society" as it was in the "old" national economy. Only one aspect of this argument may be relevant: the need to expand through distance education and Internet-based training, the access and capabilities of adults to take advantage of the cybernetic digital culture.

Few models of adult learning education take seriously the Faure Report's motto of promoting learning from the cradle to the grave, and organize ALE along a continuum from kindergarten to post-secondary education to leisure activities for the Third Age. The fact is that the highest-paying jobs go to people with more education and that new jobs tend to be concentrated in the service sector, some of which require more sophisticated knowledge more likely to be acquired through practice rather than through formal training beyond general post-secondary education. This is apparent in the rarefied atmosphere of Southern California's more sophisticated sectors (such as highly paid personal trainers for Hollywood movie stars) as well as in other less complex, less well-paid areas (child and elder caretakers, gardeners, etc.).

There is no reason to believe that neoliberal globalization will offer new opportunities for governmental politics in the area of adult learning education. However, there is sufficient evidence, on a global level, that social movements can persist in the tradition of struggle, reinforcing a fierce level of commitment in support of and on the part of the disadvantaged classes. Likewise, it is predictable that the reorganization of the world system may take place around a State-centric model of political and economic capital accumulation. If this new model resembles to a certain extent a return to reconstituted models of the welfare state, this process may open unique avenues for the inception of new models of adult learning education.

In terms of international rhetoric and discourse, there is little debate about the importance of adult lifelong learning education and training in contemporary societies. What is still a matter of important academic and political debate is how ALE could more expeditiously contribute to equity, equality of opportunity, and quality of education in formal, non-formal, and informal education settings. Similarly, what type of learning are we advocating under the label of lifelong learning, including issues of quality, relevance, and pertinence of adult learning education knowledge? Finally, how can we proceed to evaluate the impacts of the potential recommendations of CONFINTEA VI for the next decade of adult education development? These are all valuable questions, but I will not respond to all of them, as such a feat would be impossible in the context of a short book like this one. However, I would like to focus on how we can unleash the power of adult learning education in the face of the complex civilization crises that we are experiencing, the subject of Chapter Four.

NOTES

[1] As Rauno Huttunen explains, "Indoctrination means infiltrating (drilling, inculcating, etc.) concepts, attitudes, beliefs and theories into a student's mind by passing her free and critical deliberation" (Op. Cit. p. 1).

[2] Perhaps it is opportune to remind ourselves of Marx's dictum that no social form dies and disappears altogether, but that while new social formations are being created, the old social formations still survive for a while, creating a more heterogeneous, conflictive, and occasionally chaotic modes of production. See Marx, K. (1977). *A contribution to the critique of political economy.* Moscow: Progress Publishers.

[3] I choose the response to the G-7 meeting in Genoa because of the graphic experience of a political activist, Carlo Guliani who was murdered by the police in front of the world mass media. Yet, there is no question that confrontation to the model of neoliberalism propelled by the G-7 or G-8 has grown, as has grown the opposition to the Davos annual meetings of the most powerful corporative and government elites. The World Social Forum and the World Educational Forum, which originated in Brazil but now have a global reach, represent one of such concerted responses to a more "globalized" political elite, characterized by many as a global plutocracy.

CHAPTER IV

ADULT LEARNING EDUCATION AND
CIVILIZATION CRISES

"Our civilization ... is a civilization which has destroyed the simplicity and repose of life; replaced its contentment, its poetry, its soft romance dreams and vision with the money-fever, sordid ideals, vulgar ambitions, and the sleep which does not refresh."[1]

This chapter addresses how adult learning education may contribute to our modern societies, signaling what I have termed the crises of our modern civilization. There is no question that we are facing a profound set of intertwined crises, and that they seem to feed to each other. In facing this challenge we need to delve into the richest pedagogical and political contributions of adult learning education's historical legacies.

What contributions could adult learning education make to the changing world system (e.g. the post-neoliberal models that are emerging in a possible State-centric orientation)? What contributions could adult learning education make to advance a learning society and the knowledge society? How do we deal with the political, social, and ecological development models that so far have been termed as globalizations but that could easily be reframed as planetarization?

The challenges are daunting. We should follow the best insights of many who had made substantial and robust contributions to ALE, including Paulo Freire, Everett Reimer, Miles Horton, John Dewey, Jean Jacques Rousseau, Mary Wollstonecraft, Rigoberta Menchú, Franz Fanon, Amilcar Cabral, the Folk High School Movement and Nikolaj Frederik Severin Grundtvig, Ivan Illich, Rosa Parks, Martin Luther King, Lanza del Vasto, Malcon Knowles, Jack Mezirow, Antonio Gramsci, Theilard de Chardin, Edward Lindeman, Moacir Gadotti, and Ari Antikainen, to name a few. Together they have offered insightful discussions of how adult learning education can contribute to active participation, active citizenship, and active learning throughout life in politics, economy, culture, and society.

We cannot in the brief space of this chapter review, summarize, synthesize, analyze, criticize, and propose narratives and alternatives by reviewing the contributions of these giant thinkers who have made enormous contributions to the development of adult learning education. There is certainly a role for Ph.D. dissertations to analyze the contributions of these thinkers and scholars, giants of social and educational thought. Nonetheless, government officials, graduate and undergraduate students, professors and teachers, researchers, militants of the social movements and NGOs, adult learning education practitioners, and the common citizen, will all be well

47

served by reading and reflecting upon the contributions of scholars and visionaries such as those listed above, along with many others. The above list is by no means exhaustive.

A Scenario of Crises: Crisis is Opportunity

Sinologists have long documented that in the Chinese writing the sign for crisis is identical to the sign for opportunity. "Crisis is opportunity," may be considered an optimistic reading facing civilizational crises in the spirit of the Chinese grammar. The Chinese translation of "Crisis is opportunity" is 危機即是轉機, meaning that crisis is the turning point and that it may bring good chance or opportunity to the future.

There is a fundamental tension in modern civil and political societies between regulation and emancipation. In addition to these secular tensions, modern societies are confronting multiple crises, including but not restricted to a moral crisis, a crisis of regulation (sometimes referred as the ingovernability of democracies), a fiscal crisis of the State, a financial mega-crisis bringing about the demise of neoliberalism as the guiding light of globalization, a crisis of emancipation and solidarity, a planetary crisis of the environment, a crisis of productivity in solidarity, a crisis in the politics of culture related to immigration and multiculturalism, and an epistemological crisis.

For the purposes of this chapter, five key crises have been identified and will be discussed: namely a moral crisis; the crisis of neoliberalism; the crisis of human rights, immigration, and multiculturalism as the bedrock of citizenship; the planetary crisis; and the epistemological crisis. Adult learning education could make robust contributions to ameliorate if not to solve these civilization crises in the near future.

1. A moral crisis There is a serious moral crisis in capitalist societies. We are reminded of this moral crisis by the constant reference to the "moral hazard" or the risk to help, with the plan of the salvation of banks in the recent financial mega-crisis, those bankers, speculators, managers and financiers who brought about the crisis in the first place through unethical speculation and shady financial instruments. They made fortunes in the process, leaving the taxpayers to foot the bill of rescuing the financial institutions, in particular the banking system.

A large number of youth, children, and adults have been experiencing these crises at several levels in their lives. There is also a most serious conflict of ethnicities, religious beliefs, class, gender, and of course racial exchanges in our educational institutions and practices, and that is also aggravating the way children, youth, and adults cope with the moral and cognitive crises that they experience in their societies. Lost in the struggle for meaning and identity is the same notion of tolerance that we have indulged as one of the premises of the Enlightenment, and some political scientist will also argue, the governability of democracies.

There are many other symptoms of this crisis, such as pervasive corruption in many public sectors; the lack of transparency and checks and balances in the business world revealed by the extraordinary gaps in remunerations between the employers and the CEOs of a given company, or what has been indicated with the greedy and predatory business practices that led to the macro-financial crisis; the presence and action of narco-trafficking as parallel power in many societies; the merchants of arms feeding militias of many ideological signs; wars predicated as a preemptive self-defense against arms of massive destruction that were never found; or the systematic annihilation of populations and genocides such as the most recent experience of Darfur. Unfortunately, examples abound in today's societies.

Cornel West talks about this crisis, speaking of an undeniable cultural decay in the United States that frightens him more than anything else: "By unprecedented cultural decay, I mean the social breakdown of the nurturing system for children. The inability to transmit meaning, value, purpose, dignity, and decency to children" (West, 1996, p. 196).

In the spirit of West, we should be reminded of the thoughts of Dante Alighieri who, in the *Divine Comedy, The Book of the Inferno*, claims that God has reserved the darkest places in hell for those who maintain their neutrality at times of moral crisis.[2]

2. The crisis of neoliberalism Neoliberal governments promote notions of open markets, free trade, the reduction of the public sector, the decrease of state intervention through regulations in the economy and the deregulation of markets. As Michael Apple (1993) has stated in several of his own works, neoliberalism and neoconservativism are two sides of the same coin. While neoliberalism emphasizes the economic characteristics of a model of global capitalist hegemony, neoconservatism offers, as an addendum, which is not contradictory to the above stated principles, a set of moral and ethical codes, which dovetail quite nicely with the principles of neoliberalism. This agenda includes a drive towards privatization and decentralization of public education, a movement toward educational standards, and the testing of academic achievement to determine the quality of education at the level of students, schools, and teachers. Accountability is another key tenet of the model. The financial and policy prescriptions of neoliberalism are now being challenged with a reorganization of the world system, and predictably, it will have impacts on the politics of culture and education.

Research on globalization and education involves the study of intertwined worldwide discourses, processes, and institutions affecting local educational practices and policies. The four major theoretical perspectives regarding globalization and education are world culture, world systems, postcolonial, and culturalist. The major global educational discourses are about the knowledge economy and technology, lifelong learning, global migration or brain circulation, and neoliberalism. The major institutions contributing to global educational discourses and actions are the World Bank, the Organization for Economic Cooperation and Development (OECD), the World Trade Organization and its General Agreement on Trade in Services (GATS), the United Nations, and UNESCO.

Neoliberal discourses and GATS have stimulated a push for global privatization of educational services, particularly in higher education and the sale of information services and books by multinational corporations. There are also global intergovernmental organizations and nongovernmental organizations resisting the dominant global discourses by promoting educational agendas based on human rights and environmentalism. International testing, particularly TIMSS and PISA, contribute to the growing global uniformity of national curricula. Instruction in English is becoming a standard feature of national curricula as result of it being the language of global commerce. Gender equality in education is a priority of most global organizations.

Critics of current neoliberal global trends support educational alternatives that will preserve local languages and cultures, ensure progressive educational practices that will protect the poor against the rich, continue striving for gender parity in education, and protect the environment and human rights.

A central premise of my analysis, developed in several publications (Torres, 2009a, 2009b) is that globalization processes influence educational reform in the Third World in different ways. Yet, neoliberal globalization is not wholly hegemonic, pervasive, all encompassing or uncontested at the local and global level. Likewise, while I insist that in terms of policy orientations the age we are now living is the age of neoliberalism, it does not, as does any hegemonic model, go uncontested, nor has it demonstrated itself to be technically and, more importantly, politically, capable of ruling with an "iron fist" that cannot be challenged or defeated. As the election of Lula replacing the experience of the neoliberal government of Fernando Henrique Cardoso in Brazil, or many other instances in Latin America like the models put forward by the governments of Venezuela, Ecuador, Bolivia, and Argentina has shown, neoliberalism may lose legitimacy and the power to govern (Morrow & Torres, 1995; Torres, 2002a, 2002b, 2002c).

3. A crisis of human rights, immigration, and multiculturalism as the bedrock of citizenship Today the question of immigration related to multiculturalism and citizenship has taken center stage:

> Immigration represents the emerging aspects, probably the most evident, of the wide process which characterizes more and more the whole planet— globalization. Migrations represent more than a phenomenon, a historical certainty that can be found today, though with different features, in all countries and, in particular, in the most developed. Migration phenomena are becoming more and more important within the Mediterranean basin. (Foundazione Laboratori Mediterraneo, 1997, cited by Mayo, 2005, p. 110).

The question of human rights in education has become a central question for citizenship and democracy, and indeed for education. Nuhoglo Soysal's analysis of the limits of citizenship in the era of globalization highlights some of these issues. She argues that "the logic of personhood supersedes the logic of national citizenship

[and] individual rights and obligations, which were historically located in the nation state, have increasingly moved to an universalistic plane, transcending the boundaries of particular nation-states" (Soysal, 1994, pp. 164–165).

Soysal's analysis of the limits of citizenship has implications at three levels: first, at the level of citizenship, where notions of identity and rights are decoupled; second, at the level of the politics of identity and multiculturalism, where the emergence of membership in the policy "is multiple in the sense of spanning local, regional, and global identities, and which accommodates intersecting complexes of rights, duties and loyalties," and finally, given the importance of the international system for the attainment of democracy worldwide, the emergence of what could be termed cosmopolitan democracies, that is, international political systems relatively divorced in their origin and constitute dynamics from the nation-states' codes (Soysal, 1994, p. 166).

For instance, critical stances to human rights from feminist perspectives criticize the concept per se, because "It's Western, it's male, it's individualistic, its emphasis has been on political and not economic rights" (Bunch, 2001, pp. 138–139). Yet, despite these criticisms, human rights are seen as "a powerful term that transforms the discussion from being about something that is a good idea to that which ought to be the birthright of every person" (Bunch, 2001, pp. 138–139).

If the agenda for human rights is reconfiguring the boundaries of nations and individual rights of national citizens, and they are seen as a precondition to attain basic equality worldwide, the educational systems and adult learning education will reflect, more and more, the tension between human rights as a globalized ideology of cosmopolitan democracies, and the growing nationalistic feeling in many educational systems that were built as powerful tools of the Enlightenment. This tension is also projected in questions of identity and the rights of cultural and religious values to be upheld independently of the ideology of human rights and its demands upon educational systems. Once again, adult learning education has a major role to play vis a vis identity, multiculturalism, human rights, and citizenship.

4. A planetary crisis   The discussion about a planetary crisis seems to be an non-sequitur following the policy debates and empirical evidence on global warming, pesticides as water pollutants, exhaustions of natural non-renewable resources, the thinning of the ozone layer, the greenhouse effect, the food crisis and desertification of several areas of the globe particularly in the Sub-Saharan Africa, the disappearance of plants and animals, as well as the growing endangerment of species or the devastation of the Amazons and tropical rain forests. In one sentence, the planetary crisis relates to the difficulties of establishing lasting foundations for a sustainable development of the planet.

UNESCO's own distribution packet for the United Nations declared 2005–2014 the Decade of Education for Sustainable Development. Gustavo Lopez-Ospina used the definition from the 1997 Brundtland Commission as "caring for the needs of the present without compromising the possibility for future generations to satisfy their own needs" (Lopez-Ospina, 2003, p. 42).

Mahadevia (2001) states that the following elements need immediate attention for sustainable development in the South: "sustainable livelihoods; secure housing rights; and freedom from violence and intimidation on the basis of social identity" (p. 78). Macro-level sustainable development must ensure "(i) effective government policies to reduce inequality within cities themselves and between the rural and urban areas; (ii) democratic urban development processes that meet the needs of the disadvantaged, and in which the most disadvantaged can participate; (iii) economic growth through activities that are non-polluting and labor-intensive; (iv) a sound, participatory regulatory mechanism to check unsustainable activities; and (v) government responsibility for promoting human development" (Mahadevia, 2001, p. 78).

The most simple definition of sustainable development can be found in the report *Our Common Future*: "sustainable development is a transformation process in which the use of natural resources, the direction given to investments, the orientation given to technological development and institutional change get in harmony with each other and reinforce the present and future potential, in order to fulfill human needs and aspirations" (CMMAD, 1988) As we can see, sustainable development is a very wide concept. The report does not give details, which has been the source of much ambiguity, "leaving the concept open to creativity and ideological disputes" (Gadotti, 2008, p. 20).

5. An epistemological crisis The crisis of epistemology is brought about by the crisis of positivism as normal and hegemonic science, arguing that science is independent from culture. This dovetails quite nicely with the premise in most educational establishments that education is independent from politics. The challenge to these two hypotheses will entail a long and detailed discussion of the foundations of science in contemporary society. Suffice is to say that many scholars have argued that the cultural assumptions of normal science are not neutral, and that one may question the degree, process, and methods to achieve objectivity in science. It is not necessary to embrace the arguments of Foucault linking science to power to argue that science is never neutral. Thomas Popkewitz (1988) says it quite well:

> The view of society as composed by 'possessive' individuals provides a basis for organizing schooling. Attitudes, knowledge, and skills are conceived of as the personal property of the individual. The psychology of a possessive individual is incorporated into contemporary curriculum through the use of behavioral objectives, notions of affective and cognitive learning, taxonomies of knowledge and processes, and psychological testing and measurement. Methods of teaching are to enable individuals to develop particular attributes and abilities and to internalize some logical state which they 'own' as one would objects or commodities. (p. 86)

Positivism emerged in the nineteenth century as a position that stressed the unity of the logic of science; consequently there was no basis for a methodological differentiation between the natural and the social sciences. Classic positivists defended the natural scientific model of causality and invariant laws as the logical basis of all inquiry. This approach has been challenge by a variety of approaches, more so in adult learning education (Morrow & Torres, 1995, p. 43).

Positivistic notions of knowledge are built on a growing accumulation of facts rather than a perception of the world characterized by discontinuities and small results with gradual consequences. Another disputable aspect of positivistic research is the notion of ownership of knowledge, which results from research being commissioned and financed by organizations that retain control over the results. The idea of value-free research, sponsoring the neutrality and apoliticity of the researcher, and the goal to measure, represent, and analyze every inch of human action with a value-free methodology is another of the keystones of positivism.

The result is what Boaventura de Souza Santos, following seventeenth century philosopher Gottfried Leibniz calls "indolent reasons," which is both metonymic and proleptic. Drawing from a vast array of literary figures, de Sousa Santos argues that this "indolent reason" is metonymic, employing a figure of speech consisting of the use of the name of one thing for that of another of which it is an attribute or with which it is associated, hence taking the part as the whole. It is proleptic, following another literary strategy, because the narrator knows the ending of the novel but will not tell us, the reader. The metonymic is extremely reductive, while the proleptic nature of indolent reasons makes the future infinite, that is, it is expanded without limits.

Hence, particularly in the Western knowledge, this indolent reasons produces what de Sousa Santos describes as monocultures: the monoculture of knowledge and rigor (that only scientific knowledge is rigorous knowledge), the monoculture of lineal time (the idea that history has a direction, a sense, and that the developed societies lead the pack), the monoculture of naturalization of differences (hiding classifications through naturalization hierarchies, that is racial and ethnic classification, sexual classification, gender classification, caste classification, etc.), the monoculture of the dominant scale (where the universal and global emerges as dominant and hegemonic, and the local and particular remains invisible or discardable), and the monoculture of capitalist production (seen as the only way to produce).

Against these monocultures, de Sousa Santos proposes ecology of wisdom. This means science in dialogue with the popular cultures, the lay cultures, with indigenous knowledge, with elders' knowledge, with the *campesino* and urban marginal knowledge. This also implies an ecology of multiple times, including the voice of our ancestors. Then de Sousa proposes an ecology of recognition, employing post-colonial approaches to decolonize the minds. He also proposes an ecology of multiple scales, assuming the differences in the local, regional, national, continental, and global. Finally, he envisions an ecology of productivity, recuperating traditional and alternatives models and methods of production.[3]

Thus the lingering question is how adult learning education could help to confront, and eventually solve, some of these civilization crises – obviously not as an independent policy or field but as part of a more complex development model. I will argue that we need to unleash the power of adult learning education to reclaim the dream of liberation.

NOTES

[1] Mark Twain, *Letters from the Earth,* cited in C.A. Torres (1998). *Democracy, education and multiculturalism: Dilemmas of citizenship in a global world.* (p. 167). Lanham, MD: Rowman and Littlefield.

[2] Quote retrieved from http://www.memorable-quotes.com/dante+alighieri,a2027.html.

[3] See de Sousa Santos, B. (2003). The World Social Forum: Towards a counter-hegemonic globalization. Part of a paper presented at the XXIV International Congress of the Latin American Studies Association, Dallas, March 27–29. Retrieved from http://www.choike.org/documentos/wsf_s318_sousa.pdf.

CHAPTER V

REINVENTING ADULT LEARNING EDUCATION: UNLEASHING THE POWER, RECLAIMING THE DREAM

The culture of science that predominates in many academic circles dissociates almost by definition science from culture, and analytics from advocacy. While there are portentous analytical risks when advocacy is brought to the fore as a central element of educational policy formation and some institutions like UNESCO have assumed explicit responsibilities in this regard — advocacy is almost a non-sequitur in education.

Educational research in education cannot be dissociated from transformation and change. Unlike traditional disciplinary fields that may elaborate a complex web of concepts, methodologies, and narratives that attempt to understand, comprehend, and analyze – as well as criticize – themes, topics, and behaviors, education has an ethical and political responsibility to intervene and change the existing conditions of society. For educational research, the justification of learning for knowledge's sake while seductive is a necessary but not sufficient condition.

Educational research cannot simply be about obtaining pure knowledge because educational research faces the imperatives of transforming the reality that it studies. Moreover, educational research faces the constant challenge of linking theory, research, and praxis, as well as policy and policy implementation. Not surprisingly then, the role of advocacy is important, more so in adult learning education. Advocacy, however, should not blind the research nor should it manipulate the process and outcomes. Yet advocacy certainly needs to be recognized as part of the complexity of educational research, its ethics, its integrity, and its usefulness in transforming the lives of children, youth, adults, families, communities, and nations.

What are the emerging global challenges for adult learning education? These include poverty, environmental degradation and global warming, leisure and cultural activities for the Third Age, ecopedagogy, and the question of immigration and the enhancement of tolerance in civil societies, as well as interculturalism and multiculturalism. The last section of this chapter addresses these global challenges in detail.

It is explicitly stated in many documents discussing the role and purposes of adult learning education policies that they are supposed to work toward enhancing personal, social, and regional equality and equity. Class, race/ethnicity, sexual preference, and gender have proven to be key elements in discussing equity, equality of opportunity, and quality of education in formal, non-formal, and informal education. The end of the Cold War saw the transformation of the world into a new global economy, fueled by rapid technological transformations with faster transactions of financial capital in increasingly unregulated international capital markets. Labor and capital have increased mobility across borders, justifying a commonplace assessment by journalists that the world is flat (Friedman, 2006). Yet the recent macro-financial crisis may be redefining the way the global economy works in meaningful and drastic ways.

Another fundamental challenge for adult learning education is fostering democracy and multiculturalism, based on a model of human rights and global citizenship. The leitmotif here is the Latin adage "ad fontes." How did all of this start? What was the grand design behind the creation of the United Nations system, of UNESCO, and of adult education? Adult education emerged immediately after the Second World War as a result of the constitution of the United Nations system, and particularly UNESCO. The central preoccupation was how to advance the cause of democracy through pedagogical means to prevent another fascism from emerging and how to educate the population at large in the civic culture of democracy as stated in the classic book by Almond and Verba (1963).

With the horror of war devastation, the concentration camps and the gas chambers for the "final solution," most of the victorious governments after the war concluded that there was a tremendous contradiction in how some of the most advanced nations in the world (Italy and Germany, for instance), which had developments in the arts, sciences, philosophy, and music unmatched by most countries, could have germinated such irrational and belligerent model of policy and governance as fascism.

The question of State authoritarianism immediately connected with the question of "authoritarian personality," the central theme of study of the Frankfurt School of Critical Theory. The answer lay somewhat in the psycho-sociological aspects of the changes in late capitalism in those societies and the breakdown of civic rules and political culture. Adult education was seen as the right answer to the dilemmas of democracy in the post-war era, and I may argue, going back to ad fontes, that this premise of building a democratic and not an authoritarian personality, still constitutes a fundamental answer to the dilemmas of democracy (and the ingovernability of democracies) in the twenty first century. Certainly the development of a democratic personality and a cosmopolitan democratic citizenship may be one of the best answers to most of the crises of civilization that we have outlined above.

There are at least two preconditions for this to be effective, that adult learning education relates to the building of a cosmopolitan democracy, and that it also collaborates in the construction of a multicultural global citizenship (Archibugi, Held, & Kohler, 1998; Torres 1998a). A good synthesis of the debates about cosmopolitan democracies and global citizenship is provided by Daniele Archibugi, which I will quote at length:

Cosmopolitan democracy is therefore a project which aims to develop democracy within nations, among states, and at the global level, assuming that the three levels, although highly interdependent, should and can be pursued simultaneously. It stresses that different democratic procedures are needed for each of these levels. Such a project proposes to integrate and limit the functions of existing states with new institutions based on world citizenship. These institutions should be entitled to manage issues of global concern as well as to interfere within states whenever serious violations of human rights are committed. World citizenship does not necessarily have to assume all the demands of national citizenship. The real problem is to identify the areas in which citizens should have rights and duties as inhabitants of the world rather than of secular states. In some cases spheres of competence may overlap, in others they would be complementary.

The cosmopolitan system envisages not only the existence of universal human rights protected by states, but also the creation of a mandatory core of rights which individuals may claim, as well as duties vis-à-vis global institutions. Rights ought to relate, in the first instance, to the sphere of survival and to issues which cross national boundaries. In relation to these rights, world citizens undersign certain duties which enable global institutions to perform a function of temporary replacement, subsidiarity and substitution vis-à-vis national institutions. (Archibugi, in Archibugi, Held, & Kohler, 1998, p. 219)

However, the complexities of societies and forms of social action in the constitution of civil societies invite us to revisit in this section the growing importance of social movements, community organizations, NGOs, and public intellectuals in fostering a democratic culture and practices that enrich our lives, excite our senses, and help build the bedrocks of tolerance and solidarity, which are, jointly with human rights and sustainable development, the pillars of a healthy and workable democratic pact.

Unleashing the Power of Adult Learning Education

"Adult educators are never neutral. They are cultural activists committed to support and extend those canons, social practices, institutions, and systems that foster fuller free participation in reflective discourse, transformative learning, reflective action, and a greater realization of agency for all learners. Justification for the norms derived from these commitments is continually open to challenge through critical discourse."[1]

The question is this: How can we work toward a convergent vision of adult learning education that is technically competent, ethically sound, spiritually engaging, and politically feasible?

The final section of this chapter provides a set of foundations for ALE to emerge as a paradigm of emancipation and empowerment, and a politically feasible and ethically solid answer to the civilization crises discussed above.

RETHINKING, UN-THINKING, AND REINVENTING ADULT LEARNING
EDUCATION FOR EMANCIPATION AND EMPOWERMENT

*1. For a New Epistemology: Adult Learning Education as
a Critique of Obscurantism*

"The day that the forces of power and domination which govern science and technology are able to discover a way to kill intentionality and the active character of consciousness which makes consciousness perceptible to itself, we will no longer be able to speak of liberation. But precisely because it is not possible to kill or blot out the creative, re-creative and receptive force of consciousness, what do those in command do? They mystify reality because, as there is no reality other than the reality of consciousness, when the reality of consciousness is mystified the consciousness of reality is mystified as well. And by mystifying the consciousness of reality, the process of the transformation of reality is obstructed."[2]

There is no reason for our definition of obscurantism to be related to the definition of obscurantism from the Middle Ages. As Jacques Le Goff defines with tremendous clarity, the Middle Ages planted the seeds of modernity. This famous medievalist affirms, "Those that speak of obscurantism have not comprehended anything. Obscurantism is a false idea, linked to the Enlightenment and to Romanticism. The modern era was born in the medieval. The struggle for laicism – the independence of the state from church interference – in the nineteenth century contributed to the legitimization of the idea that the deeply religious Middle Ages were obscurities. The truth is that the Middle Ages was an age of faith, stimulated by the search for reason. To this we owe the State, the nation, the city, the university, individual rights, women's emancipation, the conscience, the organization of war, the mill, the machine, the compass, the hour, the book, purgatory, confession, the proprietor, the alter cloth, and even the French Revolution."[3]

The obscurantism to which we are referring is that which Freire insinuates in his criticism of dominant power. This obscurantism results from the manipulation of the media, from the construction of state administration and public policy as domination and not as service to the common good, and from the manipulation of science and technology in order to dominate, oppress, exploit, and subjugate the population. This public lie is a way of obtaining private benefits. This is the constant distortion and disinformation which was in the best style of the Medieval Ages, perhaps comparable to the logic of the Crusades for the reconquering of Jerusalem, unleashing a just war in Iraq to avoid proliferation of weapons of mass destruction that were never found.

There is also the obscurantism of science, where positivism as the dominant scientific logic "has transformed from pure scientism into a strategy of technical control based in methodological individualism that harmoniously converges with the logic of the market and with the states that seek to adapt themselves to that logic" (Morrow & Torres, 2004, p. 9).

The antidote to obscurantism of power is the double "key" of critical consciousness, which is, on the one hand, an epistemology of curiosity as Freire proposes, constantly questioning, feeling unsatisfied with the answers, not leaving anything outside the range of questioning, using candor and the simplicity of a child's gaze to inspect even the most intricate relationships and experiences. On the other hand, critical consciousness is an epistemology of suspicion, following Freirean thought and that of the great French phenomenologist Paul Ricoeur.

This is a suspicion that all human interaction and all human experience – to the extent that they involve power relations – involve relations of domination and must therefore be subject to a systematic critique. If this is applicable to the interaction between individual people (children and their parents, children and their teachers, interfamilial relationships) it is even more applicable to the interactions between people and institutions. Because of this it is reasonable to affirm that this epistemological model of suspicion reveals how the logic of capital and especially the logic and the rights of private property tend to prevail, in practice and legally, over the logic and the rights of the people

2. Adult Learning Education in Support of an Alternative Globalization: Planetarization

In the context of the struggle against neoliberal globalization, the response lies in promoting a respectful and dignified planetarization, of men and women of the planet, based on an ethic of work, communication, and solidarity, but also on an ethic of production that isn't based on greed, avarice, or usury. Moacir Gadotti said it very well:

Opening the school to the world, as Paulo Freire wanted, is one of the conditions for schools to survive with dignity at the start of the new millennium. The new space for school is the planet, because the earth has been transformed into our home for all. The new educational paradigm is based on the planetary condition of human existence. Planetarianism is a new category on which the earth paradigm is based, that is, the utopistic vision of the earth as a living and evolving organism where human beings organize themselves into one community, sharing the same dwelling place with other beings and with other things.[4]

3. Adult Learning Education in Support of Eco-pedagogy[5]

The pedagogy of the Earth, as Moacir Gadotti titled one of his notable books, should be the pedagogy that inspires all pedagogy: ecopedagogy. Indeed, Gadotti affirms:

The classic paradigms, based on a predatory anthropocentric and developmentalistic industrialist vision, are becoming worn out, as it is not able to explain the present moment nor respond to future needs. We need another paradigm, based on a sustainable vision of the planet Earth. Globalism is essentially unsustainable, caring first about the needs of capital and afterward about human needs. And many of the human needs about which globalism cares become 'human' just because they were produced as such to serve capital.[6]

Ecopedagogy invites one to reflect upon ecology and the image of the social movements that work toward preserving the environment, clean air, uncontaminated groundwater, the forests (the lungs of the planet), the birds, animals, insects, and plants that inhabited the planet before us and on which we greatly depend for our subsistence and for curing our illnesses. Clearly, ecopedagogy also invites one to reflect upon the image of preventing the pillaging of natural resources, especially those that are nonrenewable as the great Brazilian theologian Leonardo Boff suggests.

As the Spanish environmentalist and carpenter Ignacio Abella states, defining himself as someone who "learned to walk with amazement," (2000; 2003) only those who can be amazed at the magnificence of nature can respect it, appreciate it, and become passionate about it and its protection – which is also the protection of our future, our children, and our grandchildren.

Ecopedagogy is a pedagogy focused in life: It takes into account people, cultures, lifestyles, and respect of identity and diversity. It acknowledges human beings as creatures that are always in movement, as "incomplete and unfinished" beings, according to Paulo Freire who are constantly shaping themselves, learning, and interacting with others and with the world.

Ecopedagogy and education for sustainability are closely linked. As Gro Harlem Brundtland wrote in the preface of the United Nations report *Our Common Future*, "Unless we are able to translate our words into a language that can reach the minds and hearts of people young and old, we shall not be able to undertake the extensive social changes needed to correct the course of development." This is one of the tasks of the education for sustainability."[7]

It is important to point out, as Alicia Bárcena (1989) does in the preface of Francisco Gutiérrez and Cruz Prado's book *Ecopedagogia e Cidadania Planetaria*, that the construction of an environmental citizenship is a strategic component for the process of building a democracy. In her opinion, environmental citizenship is truly a planetary one, since, within the ecological movement, local and global spheres are interlinked. The deforestation of the Amazon forest or of any forest in the world is not a simply local fact. It is an act of violence against planetary citizenship. Ecologism has many recognized merits when addressing the theme of planetarity; this movement was a pioneer in the extension of the concept of citizenship in the context of globalization and also in the practice of a global citizenship in such a way that nowadays global citizenship and ecologism are part of the same social action field, with common aims and sensibilities.[8]

And here is the contribution that can be given by the Earth Pedagogy, the ecopedagogy. Francisco Gutiérrez and Cruz Prado (1989) remind us that ecopedagoy is a pedagogy that intends to promote learning the "sense of things, departing from our daily lives." We discover the sense of things within the process, by living the context and opening new paths. That is why it is a democratic and solidarity pedagogy (Gadotti, 2008, p. 18).

Thus, ecopedagogy as a planetarian model confronts the perspectives of "deep" ecology versus "shallow" ecology: "Deep ecology directly problematizes the relationship between environment and society. It conceptualizes the human species as in a relationship of domination over nature, and suggests that human exploitation of the environment is currently precipitating a crisis in environment-society relations. We have damaged the environment to such a catastrophic extent that radical and drastic measures are necessary to halt such destruction, and this requires that we change the way we conceptualize nature" (Cudworth, 2003). Moreover: "Deep ecologists argue that we must move from human-centeredness or 'anthropocentrism' as the key structuring principle of social organization to a nature-orientated 'biocentric or ecocentric' principle" (Naess, 1990, p 135).

On the contrary, a shallow ecology endorses values, which are largely economic and unproblematic. The implications of sustainable development for the moral/social/political structure of society are basically consistent with the status quo. Understood in this way, sustainable development rapidly converges with common sense and instrumental rationality determines the means for achieving a set of taken-for-granted ends (Bonnett, 2003, p. 12).

Some proponents of ecopedagogy would agree that capitalism as a form of production will always need markets. But as a form of social organization capitalism could become "green capitalism" under the assumption that markets can operate with motives other than competition for profit maximization in mind. Consumers are not to be concerned with "quality" and "value for the money" but with avoiding products adversely affecting Third World countries or causing unnecessary waste by over-packaging, etc. (Cudworth, 2003, p. 82; Gollanez, 1988, p. 5).

4. Adult Learning Education in Support of an Education for Social Justice Challenging the Principles of Neoliberalism

Education for social justice constitutes the antithesis of the model of neoliberal globalization. Education for social justice is a theoretical paradigm that inspires teacher formation and pedagogical practice and that ought to inspire not only curriculum and instruction – that is, the model of teaching learning – but also the formulation of educational policy. Why is social justice able to resist neoliberal globalization? In the abbreviated space of this chapter, I want to point out a few reasons.[9] Within the larger proposal, social justice encompasses the following aspects:

a. education as social justice explores, analyzes, and criticizes the inequalities that exist among people;
b. through the study of the resources available to communities, families, students, social activists, and social movements, education for social justice questions the

possessive individualism proposed by neoliberal globalization as well as the basis of the support of the logic of avarice and greed over social factors;

c. through education for social justice we look to give power to the people through knowledge, knowledge that must pertain to the general public. Hence the discussion of "open sources" in the construction of computer programs and in the notion of public domain of knowledge—MIT has posted all the syllabi of its courses on the internet for anybody to access;

d. education for social justice resists that notion of educational mercantilization or what is known in political economy as commodification, i.e., turning children, youth, and adults into merchandise valued for their use values and exchange values. That is, education for social justice defends a principle of citizenship education instead of an education for those consumers who can pay. Citizens have rights and obligations. Consumers have above all rights and only one obligation: to consume.

There is then the option of employing a "capability approach" as outlined by Manzoor Ahmed (2008):

> Nobel prize-winning economist Amartya Sen has been the proponent of the capability approach as the framework for conceptualizing and evaluating the ideas of social justice, individual wellbeing and education. The capability approach has emerged as an alternative to standard economic frameworks for thinking about poverty, inequality and human development generally. Sen looks upon education as the means to expand human capabilities, freedom, choice and agency. The capability approach provides a powerful rationale for lifelong learning as the conceptual underpinning for educational development goals and strategies. (p. 61)[10]

5. Adult Learning Education in Support of a Multicultural and Cosmopolitan Citizenship

Todd Gitlin cautious us that: "The question is how to cultivate the spirit of solidarity across the lines of difference — solidarity with anyone who suffers. For surely that spirit cannot be expected to generate spontaneously inside fortified groups, each preoccupied with refining its differences from other groups" (Gitlin, 1995, p. 217).

A true planetary citizenship is cosmopolitan in nature. Here then we encounter the Kantian dilemma: How is it possible to create a democracy in a country when the country is part of an international system that is not democratic, yet at the same time, how is it possible to establish an international democratic system when many of the national entities that make up the system are not themselves democratic? The struggle at the level of the international system for a multicultural citizenship of tolerance and of sensitivity that shows solidarity is another of the objectives of a radical relational approach in the struggle for human emancipation (Torres, 1998b).

6. Adult Learning Education in Support of Radical Education and Democracy

The proposal of the great pedagogues has always been a utopian proposal. Education is, in its essence, a exercise of optimism which seeks to explore the limits of the real possibilities of social transformation in search of a human sociability that inspires the progressive construction of citizens, families, communities, nations, and an international system. In this international system, reason prevails over force, peace over violence and war, justice over injustice, and over domination and oppression. This radical democratic model proposes a culture of planetary sustainability that is becoming increasingly more necessary in the face of a modernity that squanders and pillages natural resources

It is clear that education since the Enlightenment proposed, and to a lesser extent, followed through with, central objectives in the constitution of citizenship and democracy. Today, however, educators have a new responsibility, which is to be critics of culture and education. Hence educational and settings and programs should become a public sphere of deliberation, a theater of public deliberation that is neither controlled by the State nor by the market. This is a duty, a commitment, and a promise of an educational utopia to promote radical democracy (Torres, 2006, 2007a, 2007b).

7. Adult Learning Education in Support of Transecting, Transdisciplinary, and Connective Models of Knowledge

As Gadotti (n/d) affirms: The recognition of Paulo Freire outside of the field of pedagogy demonstrates that his thinking is equally transdisciplinary and transecting. Pedagogy is, essentially, a transecting science. From his first writings, Freire considered school as something much more important that the four walls which hold it up. He believed in 'cultural circles' to be an expression of this new pedagogy that was not reduced to the simplistic notion of 'classroom.' In the present community of knowledge that is much more certain, as "learning space" which is much larger than the school. The new spaces of formation (the media — radio, television, videos; churches; unions; businesses; NGOs; families; Internet, etc) extend the notion of school and the classroom. Education has become communitarian, virtual, multicultural, and ecological, and school extends to the city and to the planet. Today thinking, research, and work are done in teams without hierarchies. The notion of hierarchy (knowledge-ignorance) is held dear by the capitalistic school. On the contrary, Paulo Freire insisted on connectivity and collective management of social knowledge that comes from the bottom up. This is not just about seeing the 'Educative City' (Edgar Faure) but about catching a glimpse of the planet as a permanent school.[11]

8. *Adult Learning Education in Support of a Perspective Transformation*

The previous proposals only make sense in the context of fostering a perspective transformation in ALE. New York adult educator and professor emeritus of Teachers College-Columbia University Jack Mezirow, who is credited with creating the model of learning known as transformation theory, starts with the premise that "the human condition can be best understood as a continuous effort to negotiate contested meanings" (Mezirow, 2000, p. 3).

Thus transformation theory should "focus on how we learn to negotiate and act on our own purposes, values, feelings and meanings rather than those we have uncritically assimilated from others — to gain greater control over our lives as socially responsible, clear-thinking decision makers" (Mezirow, 2000, p. 8).

In developing a philosophy of adult education and learning, Mezirow and associates draw from a vast array of philosophical, sociological, psycho-sociological and psychoanalytical traditions (most notably Carl Jung's theory of symbolic worlds). By focusing on making meaning as a learning process, and looking at different domains of learning following Habermas' distinction between instrumental and communicative learning – outlined in the introduction of these chapters – they focus on the construction of a reflective discourse by the learners.

"Discourse, in the context of Transformation Theory, is that specialized use of dialogue devoted to searching for a common understanding and assessment of the justification of an interpretation and belief" (Mezirow, 2000, p. 10).

To achieve this level of self-reflection, perspective transformation, or transformation theory as it is known, looks for frames of reference as a meaning perspective. Frames of reference are always the result of the ways the learner interprets her or his experience. Hence, learning occurs in one of the following four ways for Mezirow and associates: "by elaborating existing frames of reference, by learning new frames of reference, by transforming points of view, or by transforming habits of mind" (Mezirow, 2000, pp. 17, 23). Indeed, we must remember that the role of adult learning educators is never neutral:

> They are cultural activists committed to support and extend those canons, social practices, institutions, and systems that foster fuller free participation in reflective discourse, transformative learning, reflective action, and a greater realization of agency for all learners. Justification for the norms derived from these commitment is continually open to challenge through critical discourse. (Mezirow, 2000, p. 30)

NOTES

[1] Jack Mezirow, Learning to Think Like an Adult. Core Concepts of Transformation Theory. In Jack Mezirow and Associates. *Learning as Transformation. Critical Perspective on a Theory in Progress.* San Francisco, Jossey-Bass, 2000, page 30.

[2] Paulo Freire, in Carlos Alberto Torres, *La praxis educativa y la acción cultural de Paulo Freire.* Valencia, Denes Editorial-Edicions del CrʰC, 2004, page 161. My translation.

[3]   Interview in *La Nación*, wednesday 12 of October 2005. http://www.lanacion.com.ar/Archivo/nota. asp?nota_id=746748.

[4]   Moacir Gadotti, La pedagogia de paulo Freire y el proceso de democratización en el Brasil. Algunos aspectos de su teoría, de su método y de su praxis. Ver también su trabajo sobre la planetarización y la cultura de la sustentabilidad Pedagogía de la tierra y cultura de la sustentabilidad. *http://www. paulofreire.org/*

[5]   See Gregery William Miiaszek, Ecopedagogia in the Age of Globalization. Educator's Perspectives of Enviromental Education Programs in the Americas which incorporate social justice models. Ph. D. dissertation Graduate School of Education and Information Studies, Los Angeles, UCLA, 2011

[6]   A ecopedagogia como pedagogia apropriada ao proceso da carta da terra. Página 1. *http://www. paulofreire.org/*

[7]   Cited by *Moacir Gadotti, Education for Sustainability: A critical contribution to the Decade of Education for Sustainable Development*. University of São Paulo, Paulo Freire Institute, São Paulo 2008, p. 5.

[8]   Moacir Gadotti, *Education for Sustainability: A critical contribution to the Decade of Education for Sustainable Development*. University of São Paulo-Paulo Freire Institute, São Paulo, 2008 p 9

[9]   These remarks have been suggested by a student who took my course of Politics and Education in UCLA, Daniel Boden "Social Justice Education as a Model to Overcome Globalization." Los Angeles, UCLA, Manuscript. 2006.

[10] For further reading, see Sen, A.K. (1992, 1999, 2005).

[11] Moacir Gadotti, La pedagogía de Paulo Freire y el proceso de democratización en Brasil. Algunos aspectos de su teoría, de su método y de su praxis. *http://www.paulofreire.org/*

ADULT LEARNING EDUCATION AND LITERACY AS INTERNATIONAL COMPARATIVE EDUCATION

"The practice of emancipatory education…is marginal to the overall adult education enterprise… for two reasons: First, adult educators have generally failed to link their efforts with movements for change, and second, agents of change have been unable to create an unified and compelling vision of the future."

(Heaney & Horton 1990, p. 91)

Lifelong learning was created to offer a unified and compelling vision of the future, and as a paradigm that would bring about change. There are three dimensions of adult learning education as a paradigm: a scientific dimension, a pragmatic dimension, and an international dimension.

The scientific dimension points to one of the major goals of adult learning education, which has been to contribute to theory building, research, and practice with the formulation of generalized propositions about the workings and the options of formal, non-formal and informal systems of learning and work apprenticeship, and their interactions with surrounding economies, politics, and cultures. Unfortunately, this dimension has been historically undermined by a field that is under-theorized compared with other fields within education, lacking systematic and substantive meta-theoretical, theoretical, and empirical research.

It should be clear that meta-theory encompasses a number of presuppositions about the constitutive parts of the world and the possibility to know them. Theories are logically deducted from meta-theories. A theory entails a number of propositions, hypotheses, and even hunches derived directly or indirectly from a meta-theory, which are not logically incompatible with the theory. Finally, empirical research is the practice of producing explanations and predictions with respect to real objects (Arnove, 2013).

The scientific dimension of the paradigm has been undermined by a number of factors, including: the lack of an abundant and highly educated cadre of researchers and teachers specializing in lifelong learning and adult learning education; the paucity of higher education programs devoting sizable resources at the undergraduate and graduate levels to train specialized adult learning education researchers, policy-planners, policymakers, and evaluators; the lack of resources provided by state institutions and to some extent by external aid organizations, to conduct research, evaluation, and experimentation in the field; and the lack of political commitment from governments to solve this conundrum. It has been said in many private conversations that the constant efforts and plight of UNESCO, as the leading international institution in this field, to reverse this situation have gone virtually unanswered. CONFINTEA VI is a splendid opportunity to resolve this conundrum and reclaim the great goals put forward by CONFINTEA V.

As a scientific perspective, adult learning education is eminently comparative, drawing from international experiences and what is known as searching for "best practices" in the field. Hence the value of combining cross-national longitudinal studies and databases with qualitative studies, participatory action research, biographical techniques, and narratives to document, analyze, and eventually calculate the benefits of lifelong learning and adult learning education programs and practices. The value of gathering comparative data, as attempted in the different regional reports of the GRALE, is in its ability to guide theory to reach reasonable propositions about the outcomes and workings of lifelong learning systems in relation to their social and historical contexts (Arnove, 2013). This of course begs a conversation about the second dimension of the paradigm.

The pragmatic dimension of adult education implies discovering what can be learned that will contribute to improving policy and practice at home. There is a process, usually referred to as "lending and borrowing," of studying and transferring educational learning experiences within a country and among countries. Yet any process of adoption or adaptation of a given "best practice" should consider a fundamental set of principles:

First, there is no one best system that fits all societies well. All systems have strengths as well as weaknesses. Moreover, many systems looks more like amalgams or conglomerates than complex functional self-reproducing systems.

Second, all educational and learning systems reflect their societies, hence there are many tensions and contradictions. Any new initiative and/or the implementation of a framework like adult learning education should be guided by knowledge of the country and/or area of implementation. Particularly in the case of adult learning education, it should be guided by knowledge of the communities where the experience will take place, knowledge of the institutions that will be in charge of the experience, familiarity with the history and unique qualities of the country, communities, grassroots organizations, and state institutions of adult learning education, and the recognition of their commonalities with other societies.

Third, all learning systems should consider the normative implications of their implementation. This implies the formulation of educational policies that are focused on the spiritual aspirations of the people, the philosophical ideas of the communities, the economic ambitions and possibilities – that is the endowments of the countries, regions, and communities – and the strengths of models of political participation and representation in the democracies.

Yet deeply embedded in the scientific dimension of lifelong learning and adult basic education is a basic principle of Education for All (EFA): that education is a human right. A note of caution is in order here. The theme of democracy runs throughout the paradigm of adult learning education, and yet the concept itself is highly contested, a sliding signifier, which means different things to different people. To be sure, an important issue is the relationship between democracy as a process and democracy as a method. An argument could be made for the need to enforce procedural democracy by creating checks and balances while eliminating clientelist and patrimonialist practices and corruption in the public sector. The dilemma is how to achieve procedural democracy while also pursuing substantive economic and political reform that will enhance the prospects for social and economic democracy. Innovations and changes in lifelong learning and adult learning education are measured for their ability to actually improve the living conditions of people and communities; for their ability to deliver cost-effective, relevant, pertinent, and timely learning experiences to the people; and for their ability to constitute a means to an end. That is to say, as outlined in the Education for All Global Monitoring Report:

Prospects for reducing poverty, narrowing extreme inequalities, and improving public health are heavily influenced by what happens in education. Progress towards the equalization of opportunity in education is one of the most important conditions to overcome social injustice, and reducing social disparities in any country. It is also a condition for strengthening economic growth; no country can afford the inefficiencies that can arise when people are denied opportunities for education because they are poor, female or members of a particular social group. And what is true at a national level also applies internationally. (Education for All Global Monitoring Report, 2008, p. 24)

Lastly, adult learning education policies and practices cannot be formulated in a historical-structural vacuum, nor can they be freely transferred from society to society without serious consideration of the social-cultural context where the experience will take place.

The international or global dimension of adult learning education is reaching a new importance with respect to the changes in the world system. Particularly when people are beginning to recognize how processes of globalization are affecting areas of the world previously considered distant, and how these in turn are affecting their own lives, families, communities, and localities. Some scholars speak of a process of globalization fueled by deep drivers (Held & McGrew, 2000, p. 243), which foreseeably will condition the institutional forms that globalization will take. These "deep drivers" include but are not restricted to:

- the changing infrastructure of global communications linked to the IT revolution;
- the development of global markets in good and services, connected to the new worldwide distribution of information;
- the pressure of migration and the movement of peoples, linked to shifts in patterns of economic demand, in demography, and in environmental degradation;
- the end of the Cold War and the diffusion of democratic and consumer values across many of the world's regions, alongside some marked reactions to this; and

– the emergence of a new type and form of global civil society, with the crystallization of elements of a global public opinion.

Discussion on globalization as a sociocultural and economic phenomenon invites some discussion about the paradigm of global education, a paradigm that has emerged over the years as a relevant analytical construct (Alger & Harf, 1986), thus it makes sense to relate the international perspective of adult learning education to the paradigm of global education. One of the key goals of the global education paradigm is to strive for a more prosperous and peaceful world, with specific roles and responsibilities attributed to education and learning, particularly to the work of teachers. An important concern for global education is the politics of culture and the need to pay attention to values, particularly how these values (local, community, regional, national, international) intersect, following or contradicting the human rights model advocated by the United Nations system.

This international perspective in adult learning education is particularly relevant for the work of adult learning education teachers and practitioners. Global education helps emphasize values and ways of seeing and acting in the world – ways that are equally valid and reflective of people's life circumstances, and also allows, in the best of the tradition of Paulo Freire and the pedagogues of liberation, to see what people have in common and how adult learning education can take advantage of the knowledge that people bring with them to the learning process. The possibility of thinking globally while acting locally also opens new perspectives to use pedagogical and didactic means to enhance learning, such as the use of art in adult learning education, or the combination of arts and crafts[1] as a learning strategy. It also opens space for the possibility of adult education teachers to educate students about the causes and consequences of the forces, dynamics, and outcomes of transnational forces, institutions, and actors. This goal should be pressed upon in teacher education programs specializing in adult learning education and in programs of literacy training, adult basic education, manpower training, apprenticeship, and undergraduate and graduate education in the field.

It is fundamental that the scientific, pragmatic, and international or global dimensions of adult learning education as a paradigm be related in such a way that the field becomes better informed and more effective in promoting educational policy and practice. There is a most important challenge in studying how various institutions, both governmental and non-governmental, as well as technical assistance agencies can better coordinate their efforts and incorporate grassroots organizations and social movements to resolve the most pressing problems of adult learning education. The African Platform for Adult Education stresses the importance of civil society in establishing these partnerships:

> Civil society organizations undertake a wide range of activities: from advocacy work to implementing programs. Sometime we are considered enemies by our government. Other times, we are the one who implements their programs. We are found in different fora either as part of our policy

dialogue or negotiation for better conditions for adult education. We also work at different levels: the community level, regional, national and international with different constituencies. But like any other organization we also have our problems and weaknesses. One of our weaknesses is our difficulty to work together, for many reasons: political differences, leadership problems and/or competition. Given the enormity of the challenges we face, it is urgent that civil society organizations bring their strengths together and jointly address these challenges. (African Platform for Adult Education, 2008, p. 20)

However, at the basic core of adult learning education is adult literacy, a special case that needs to be discussed in detail, and the focus of the following section.

The Special Case of Adult Literacy

"If before adult education literacy training was treated and carried out in an authoritarian manner, centralized in the magical comprehension of the word, a word donated by the educator to the illiterates; if before the texts generally offered for reading to student covered up much more that they revealed about reality; now, on the contrary, literacy learning as an act of knowing, as a creative act and as a political act, is an effort to read the world and the word."

(Freire, 1987, p. 35)

The EFA Monitoring Report confronts us with a startling reality: Despite a consistent international policy of struggle against illiteracy, illiteracy is still with us as a sobering reminder of a social problem that doesn't seem to go away:

An estimated 776 million adults — 16% of the world adult population — are unable to read and/or write, with understanding, a simple statement in a national or official language. Most live in South and West Asia, East Asia and Sub-Saharan Africa, and nearly two in every three are women. (EFA Monitoring, 2008, p. 93)

For the Education For All strategy, an improved rate of literacy is fundamental, since the first part of Goal #4 aims at: "Achieving a 50% improvement in levels of adult literacy by 2015, especially for women. (In terms of the reduction of the adult illiteracy rate)." Thus adult literacy rates are used as a proxy to measure progress toward EFA Goal #4.

However, the EFA Monitoring Report also shows some of the limitations of adult literacy indicators: First, the adult literacy indicator, being a statement about the stock of human capital, is slow to change and thus it could be argued that it is not a good "leading indicator" of year-to-year-progress. Second, the existing data on literacy are not entirely satisfactory. Most of them are based on "conventional" non-tested methods that tend to overestimate the level of literacy among individuals (EFA Monitoring, 2008, p. 248).

Hence, literacy measured this way is not a very reliable indicator. Being computed via "self-declaration" or third-party reporting (e.g. head of household in a national survey or household report) is rather limited. But another important limitation is that literacy (either as such or defined as functional literacy) has been adopted at the request of UNESCO as a convention that may be quite far away from the actual uses of literacy, and not representative of the actual implications of which levels and layers of literacy are needed to function effectively and productively in a given society.

UNESCO has long defined literacy as the ability to read and write, with understanding, a short simple statement related to one's daily life. However, a parallel notion arose with the introduction in 1978 of the notion of functional literacy. A definition approved in the UNESCO General Conference that year stated that a person was considered functionally literate who could engage in all activities which literacy is required for effective functioning of his or her group and community, and also for enabling him or her to continue to use reading, writing and calculation for his or her and the community's development. (EFA Monitoring, 2008, p. 2, annex)

Thus we have a problem in terms of the definition of what literacy is, and how it can be measured. But there is another conceptual problem in terms of how literacy could enhance people's lives. It is common to speak of literacy as empowering the learner. Expressions to that extent abound in the specialized bibliography and in documents produced by governments and international organizations, as well as grassroots organizations.

However, the same concept of literacy requires analysis. What does it mean to be literate, and how can the learner be empowered to be literate and be able to exercise his or her literacy? These two questions are very relevant when the different regional reports show a wide variety of definitions of what literacy is and how it can be made more effective in the context of lifelong learning and adult learning education.[2]

It will be important to dispel the myth that there is one unified form of literacy and, to speak scientifically, more specifically of several literacies. Technically, literacy training was typically considered one of the backbones of adult education, envisioning this model as a comprehensive type of education that was usually considered compensatory or "second chance" education, hence comprising literacy, adult basic education, vocational training, and community education organized as voluntary structures that were accessible to all citizens. There are complex debates in the field, but perhaps one of the most relevant asks whether literacy is a set of unitary skills related to reading, writing, and arithmetic, or if in a broader sense it encompasses a set of competencies applied to the tasks of a given culture.

Likewise, it is usually accepted that literacy is empowering by definition; however, there are important considerations to be made here because empowerment is a concept that depends on several variables. It is important to identify the "subject" to be empowered (who are the people or groups involved); the power structures connected and to which the subject will be empowered, either in agreement with or against those structures; the processes through which empowerment is sought to occur (either a top-down process, a bottom-up process, or a combination of the two), and the outcomes of the process of empowerment (which relates to questions of process and outcome) (Hickling-Hudson, 2013).

Clearly, the process of acquiring literacy is not uniform, nor is it empowering per se; people can acquire either empowering literacies, or subordinate and disempowering literacies — for instance, processes of indoctrination inducted via literacy projects conducted by authoritarian regimes.

Therefore a coherent, consistent, and convergent theory of literacy training should include different facets or domains of literacy empowerment. These include the following dimensions: basic and universal literacy, epistemic literacy, technical literacy, humanistic literacy, scientific literacy, and public literacy. Each one adds another level or potential layer of empowerment to the practice of individuals. These levels or layers do not compete but complement or even supplement each other. Finally, this distinction hints at some sort of a continuum, from basic to more advanced forms of literacy. Likewise, consideration of these various literacies can lead to important policy choices, from dominant and empowering to subordinate and disempowering.

Basic and universal literacy: This is the definition more closely related to UNESCO's conventional definition of what constitutes literacy and illiteracy. Traditionally, the ability to use reading, writing, mathematics, and computational skills with some level of efficiency to negotiate day-to-day situations was considered a benchmark of achieving basic education. The traditional liberal view of basic and universal literacy, drawing from the project of the Enlightenment, speaks of the educational relevance of a mode of understanding (through the written and not only the spoken word) the world, making pedagogy responsive to the needs of individuals. Given the complexity of today's society, this principle continues to be valuable, but needs to be considered alongside other forms of literacy. Simply to add that basic and universal literacy should lead to critical literacy is not enough, analytically or politically, as a process of empowerment.

Epistemic literacy: Learning to read and write is not enough to achieve critical and empowering literacy. It is necessary to look at the uses of written texts, and the possibility of reaching greater levels of formal knowledge, usually associated with traditional academic disciplines. It implies a set of competencies with respect to how to think about a specific problem, how to reach out for specific knowledge tools to deal with such a problem, and how to reconceptualize the problem once it has been solved. This is one of the core concepts of "Learning to Be," a model of lifelong learning expressed not only in holistic terms (human development should nurture growth of the mind and body, intelligence, sensitivity, aesthetic, and spirituality) but also as a way to develop critical thinking and judgment, and learning the tools of how to learn and how to use scientific knowledge to solve some of the riddles of everyday life.

Technical Literacy: As the term indicates, technical literacy is interpreted as ways of understanding how to apply procedural knowledge in areas of practical action.

There are different degrees of technical literacy according to the type of techniques required to achieve proficiency in a given job or working task. However, a high degree of technical literacy in the modern workplace demands competencies, skills, and abilities in a vast gamut of techniques, knowledge, and technologies based on interpreting, creating, storing, conveying, and deciphering information. Thus, Information Technology, which is one of the backbones of the proposal of a knowledge society, will have different degrees of complexity according to the different degrees of specialization and diversification of contemporary (modern or traditional) societies.

Media literacy should be considered a special case of technical literacy. Media literacy is intimately related to cultural studies, as "the schooled capacity and competency, and ability to interpret and produce media texts" (Hoeschsmann, 2006, p. 27). However, media literacy should not be conflated with news literacy (Fleming, Ph.D. dissertation, 2012).

Humanistic literacy refers to the ability of individuals to develop narratives about their own identities. That is to say, how to describe, understand, and explain the strengths and weaknesses of their own racial/ethnic, social-cultural, gender, class, and religious identities. Since language constitutes identities, humanistic literacy pays specific attention to how language organizes self-representation and reflective judgment, both individually and collectively. Intimately linked to epistemic literacy, humanistic literacy focuses on describing the development of epistemic assumptions, how those assumptions act as catalyzers in meaning-making perspectives, and how they orient social action.

Scientific literacy. Most systematic processes of formal, non-formal, and informal education and learning work toward enhancing the scientific understanding of children, youth, and adults. This understanding is about the nature and use of science for the betterment of society. This is an important goal in the context of a knowledge society. Thus, the processes of production, reproduction, transformation, innovation, and productivity associated with the workings of science (pure and applied) and of technology are foremost for development and growth. It should not be a surprise that scientific literacy, intimately associated by definition to epistemic literacy and technical literacy but encompassing a differential set of processes and outcomes, has become so important nowadays. For example, "The PISA 2006 assessment of scientific literacy among 15-year-old students offers some important lessons, for instance, a strong association between students' levels of environmental awareness and science performance" (EFA Monitoring Report, 2008, p. 37).

Public literacy. Deliberation, participation, and representation are three central components in the process of producing, sustaining, and developing a workable democracy. Public literacy is seen as the enhanced and informed ability to participate in the public sphere, while the public sphere:

Designates a theater in modern societies in which political participation is enacted through the medium of talk. It is the space in which citizens deliberate about their common affairs, hence, an institutionalized arena of discursive interaction. This arena is conceptually distinct from the state; it is a site for the production and circulation of discourses that can in principle be critical of the state.... It is not an arena of market relations but one of discursive relations, a theater for debating and deliberating rather than for buying and selling. (Fraser, 1997, p. 70)

Hence, the public sphere is a theater of public deliberation that is neither controlled by the state nor by the market. As a central component of democracy, the public sphere requires the ability of individuals who have achieved public literacy. Because of their public literacy, they are able to participate in the public sphere, understanding and creating opinion, contributing to the debate, generating seasoned and informed political, social, and economic judgments, and creating in these spaces of deliberation crucial narratives to understand and transform national, regional, community, and individual identities.

NOTES

[1]   The arts and craft movement was a British, Canadian and U.S. movement that drew from the writings of John Ruskin, with its romantic idealization of the craftsman, and opposed the mass production of industrialization developed in the latter part of the nineteenth century and the beginning of the twentieth century. It was partly a reaction to the perceived growing alienation given the development of the Industrial Revolution. The arts and craft movement impacted the transformation of architecture, decorative arts, cabinet making, crafts, and even the "cottage" garden designs. There is a loose association with religious identities such as the development of the Shaker communities that settled in the Eastern part of the United States and flourished in the nineteenth century until the Great Depression. In contemporary industrially advanced societies, a great deal of new craftsmanship related to apprenticeship programs is being influenced by the arts and craft movement, including new developments in permaculture, or adobe house movements. Most of these programs fall squarely within adult learning education programs.

[2]   For a postcolonial analysis of adult education and community development, and critique of literacy indicators, see Anne Hickling-Hudson, 2013.

CHAPTER VII

TRANSFORMATIVE SOCIAL JUSTICE LEARNING AS A NEW LIFELONG LEARNING PARADIGM: THE ROLE OF CRITICAL THEORY AND PUBLIC INTELLECTUALS

Transformative social justice learning as a social, political, and pedagogical practice takes place when people reach a deeper, richer, more textured and nuanced understanding of themselves and their world. Not in vain, Freire always advocated the simultaneous reading of the world and of the word. Based on a key assumption of Critical Theory that all social relationships involve a relationship of domination and that language constitutes identities, transformative social justice learning, from a meaning-making or symbolic perspective, is an attempt to recreate the various theoretical contexts for the examination of rituals, myths, icons, totems, symbols, and taboos in education and society, in essence an examination of the uneasy dialectic between agency and structure, setting forward a process of transformation (Torres, 2003).

From a sociological perspective, transformative social justice learning entails an examination of systems, organizational processes, institutional dynamics, rules, mores, and regulations, including prevailing traditions and customs, that is to say, key structures which by definition reflect human interest. In examining the implications of globalization for education, how can we take advantage of transformative social justice learning as a methodology and theory of social transformation? Let me be bold: one may argue that this model of transformative social justice learning is a marginal social construct in the context of contemporary social politics and that those who practice this approach are, by definition, marginal to the overall dynamics of political struggle and to the process of institutional development, in academia and elsewhere.

Politically, one may need to understand that marginality is not simply the status of being an outsider, but it also constitutes a form of insertion in the context of the global debate, and struggle, for social justice. The notion of marginality thus became a central notion in pursuing transformative social justice learning. We pursue this approach even if we know that we are marginal to the central concepts and practices of the liberal and conservative establishments (which seem to be, in education at least, poised to emphasize the need to improve cognitive learning through the movement of testing, or accountability, in schools).

Yet the idea of marginality does not rest simply on notions of opposition or negativity against the positivism, and positivity of the pedagogical, political, and epistemological models that predominate in the academy and social life. We cannot accept our marginality predicated solely on the difficulties that we face, or in the losses that we endure in this long haul, this long dureé of social struggles. We shall also celebrate, within the notion of marginality, the different triumphs that we have in our struggles. We cannot criticize without celebrating.

The notion of marginality is predicated on resorting to historically nuanced analysis of the dynamics between social agencies and structures, and on a refined conceptual understanding drawing on the strengths of Critical Social Theory. The concept of marginality is both a model of advocacy – as such it has important normative implications – and an analytical model with clear political objectives. Remember Freire's dictum: we teach on behalf of somebody and against somebody, on behalf of some values, against some values. Thus the politicity of education, a central tenet of marginality as an epistemological, political, and even spiritual position in education.

Marginality is an invitation to a struggle in the long haul, linking theory and praxis, not only as an individual but also from a social movement perspective. In so doing, a notion of marginality, and marginal voices that clamor to be heard in the debates, points to the importance of structures to help agencies. As such, reclaiming the transformative role of NGOs, teacher unions, communities, critical intellectuals, and social movements in the context of adult learning education is a must-do political practice of true marginality.

Marginality as a political and practical option draws on a model of spirituality that is clearly utopian and utopistic. It is utopian because utopia is like a distant horizon that one wants to reach but never does. You walk two steps to reach it, and it moves two steps farther. You walk two more steps, and the horizon moves two steps farther away. What is, then, the advantage of utopia as a political rationale and spiritual endeavor? It helps us to walk. Yet we draw on not only utopian but also utopistic models. We want to examine the different and alternative models of society, the utopistic models, the different social constructions that are emerging in this walking toward the future – after all, even the same notion of neoliberalism is an utopistic model, a la par, for instance, to the model of Leninism, another utopistic model of the good society.

If democracy is deliberate delusion and politics is the industry and the art of emasculating the truth, marginality became both an antidote to the ills of democracy and a suggestive methodological approach based on the principle of uncertainty – a concept that has been so well developed by physicist and Nobel Prize winner Ilya Prigogine – to achieve what many scholars, including Morris Berman, have so aptly termed the "re-enchantment of the world."

The Role of Public Intellectuals and Adult Learning Education

"There exists an international citizenship that has its rights and its duties, and that obliges one to speak out against every abuse of power, whoever the author, whoever the victim."

Michel Foucault[1]

The statement by Foucault that opens this section invites us to ponder the role of critical intellectuals. The answer from the perspective of Critical Social Theory seems to be self-evident: a true intellectual ought to be a critic of the system following the logic of determinate negation. He need not be a critic who is necessarily intransigent or intolerant by definition, but one who is able to offer to society, like a mirror, the critical aspects that need to be considered in dealing with mechanisms of sociability, production, and political exchanges. Indeed, the university as a place inhabited by intellectuals and not only by technocrats has a role to play in developing critical modes of thinking to society.

This implies, additionally, a critique of the commodification of human relations, and in the context of universities themselves, a critique of the corporatization of academic institutions as is currently outlined by the graduate employee unionization movement in the United States (Rhoads & Rhoades, 2006).

A third element is that Critical Social Theory assumes that a central role of intellectuals is to create a social imaginary – and hence, Gramsci's hypotheses about organic and traditional intellectuals (Morrow & Torres, 2004). The creation of a social imaginary implies, for critical intellectuals, a moral responsibility and a political commitment. The moral responsibility involves the imagining of social scenarios where people can deliberate and construct mechanisms of participation that may expand the workings of democracy. Or, in another fashion, a moral responsibility to extensively document through description, research, and analysis, how people build alternative methods and mechanisms of participation. Additionally, intellectuals must take on a political commitment to create a sphere of public debate, as suggested by Habermas, an autonomous sphere of public deliberation that is neither controlled by the market nor controlled by the State.

What else can be said about the role of intellectuals in the critical modernist tradition? Gramsci proposed a forceful hypothesis when he argued that everybody has the capacity to do intellectual work but only few recognize it and/or work in intellectual professions. Two key elements emerge from Gramsci's suggestion: First, intellectual work is not only a trade, a set of techniques, or a profession, but also the capacity to realize refined analysis that leads to praxis and social transformation. Secondly, a critical intellectual in the tradition of critical modernism is one who is able not only to teach but also to learn from the people, from the popular sectors. Paraphrasing Mao Tse Tung, a critical intellectual is one who is also able to capture the collective imagination of the people, in all its disorganized richness and insightfulness, and is able to return this knowledge to the people, but in a more systematic and organized fashion so that the very producers of knowledge be able to appraise, reinterpret, and rethink their own knowledge and insights, both conceptually and practically.

The production of knowledge in the human sciences is a process that involves a great deal of persuasion. Intellectuals are always trying to persuade each other, trying to show that they have a better explanation and a more powerful, far-reaching, and/or complete analysis than a previous or a competing one. From a constructivist perspective, critical intellectuals, however, are convinced that there is never a perfect or comprehensive interpretation or understanding nor a conclusive analysis that is immune from challenge or cannot be subjected to debate and criticism. Perhaps the best way to put it is the notion of Hegelian *aufhebung*: Knowledge creation is always the negation of the previous negation, the criticism of previous knowledge, which, in and by itself, is a criticism of previous knowledge and so forth.

Assuming this notion of *aufhebung* invites a sense of humility and humbleness in intellectual work. Intellectuals always work with knowledge produced by someone else – not only by individuals but by collectivities. Critical intellectuals see their work as always provisory and limited. They cannot be detached clinicians offering "objective" advice. While intellectual work is seen by conventional wisdom as eminently individual work, or the work of a team of individuals who share similar analytical, theoretical, epistemological, and methodological premises, for critical intellectuals it is collective work because it always draws from previous knowledge and from the criticism of previous knowledge. Therefore the notion of learning is as important as the notion of teaching in knowledge construction. Not surprisingly, Critical Theory has employed from its inception a multidisciplinary or interdisciplinary perspective, which is now being "discovered" by disciplinary university departments in the United States and rewarded appropriately in the evaluation of the professoriate's career developments.

Critical intellectuals assume an agonic perspective in knowledge production. Assuming that no intellectual work can provide a definitive answer to virtually any domain or problematique of the human sciences, critical intellectuals cannot, for moral and political reasons, give up the process of mutual persuasion, even if their intellectual product may be short lived. Marcuse offers a compelling argument to justify the moral dimensions of the work of critical intellectuals. Speaking, perhaps for the last time, to his disciple Jürgen Habermas, he said, "Look, I know wherein our most basic value judgment are rooted – in compassion, in our sense for the suffering of others" (cited in Habermas 1985, p. 77).

In political terms, a critical intellectual pays as much attention to the process as to the product of intellectual work – both as individual and collective endeavors. In so doing, critical modernist intellectuals remain key facilitators of intellectual exchanges in the production of collective symbolism and rituals. They remain key to facilitating the creation of spaces for public conversation, as Paulo Freire has exemplified throughout his own life. A few years ago, I was interviewing Freire and asked him what he would like his legacy to be. He answered that when he died, he would like people to say of him: "Paulo Freire lived, loved, and wanted to know." Freire, in his poetic style, provided a simple and yet powerful message about the role of critical intellectuals. For Freire, critical intellectuals should live passionately their own ideas, building spaces of deliberation and tolerance in their quest for knowledge and empowerment. They love what they do, and those with whom they interact. Love, then, becomes another central element of the political project of intellectuals agonizing in producing knowledge for empowerment and liberation.

Finally, it is their love for knowledge itself that makes them sensitive to popular knowledge and common sense. Following Gramsci, critical intellectuals know that common sense always has a nucleus of "good sense." From this "good sense" of the common sense, critical intellectuals can develop a criticism of conventional wisdom, knowledge, and practices. In educational policy and planning, this "good sense" could be a starting point for a critique of instrumental rationalization. In this context, critical intellectuals may resort to a political sociology of education to understand educational policy formation (Torres, 2009b).

The lessons of Critical Social Theory for adult learning education are clear and need to be remembered: politics and education intersect continually — there is an inherent politicity of education. Power plays a major role in configuring schooling and social reproduction. Social change cannot be articulated simply as social engineering from the calm environment of the research laboratory as many rational choice and game theory theorists assume — hence, the fiasco of the Iraq invasion, with President Bush declaring fully dressed as a pilot (though he never actually served in war), "Mission Accomplished." Several years later, and with thousands of American soldiers dead, the "Mission Accomplished" speech continued to haunt that Republican administration.

Social change needs to be forged in negotiations, in compromise but also in fights in the political system; it needs to be struggled in the streets with the social movements; it needs to be conquered in the schools struggling against bureaucratic and authoritarian behavior, defying the growing corporatization of educational institutions, particularly in higher education, and striving to implement substantive rationality through communicative dialogue; and it needs to be achieved even in the cozy and joyful environments of our gatherings with family and friends. Dialogue and reason cannot take vacations if one pursues the dream of social justice education and peace.

The current process of globalization if it is not simply understood as globalization from above, that is, as a neoliberal imprint, can contribute to a globalization from below (or planetarization as suggested by the Paulo Freire Institutes), to challenge some of the principles neglecting human rights and freedom in capitalist societies, henceforth enhancing the chances for cosmopolitan democracies and radical educational reform. Critical Social Theory and public intellectuals have a major role to play in the achievement of those goals.

NOTE

[1] Foucault, M. (2000). Essential works of Foucault. *Power, 3*, 474.

BIBLIOGRAPHY

Abella, I. (2004). *El Hombre y la Madera*. Barcelona, RBA-Integral.

Abella, I. (2000). *La Magia de los Arboles*. Barcelona, RBA-Integral.

Abrahamson, K. (2001). Towards new lifelong learning contracts in Sweden. In D. Aspin et al (Eds.) *International Handbook of Lifelong Learning*. Dordrecht: Kluwer.

African Platform for Adult Education (2008). Civil society report: Forging partnership towards a renewed vision of adult education in Africa. ANCEFA, FEMNET, PAALAE, PAMOJA.

Ahmed, M. (2008). Adult learning and education. Asia Pacific synthesis for the global report. (unpublished document). Hamburg.

Alger, C.F., & Harf, J.E. (1986). *Global education: Why? for whom? about what?* Columbus: Ohio State University.

Almond, G., & Verba, S. (1963). *The civic culture: political attitudes and democracy in five nations*. Sage Publications, Incorporated.

Antikainen, A. (2005). Between empowerment and control: A state intervention into participation in adult education in Finland. *European Education, 37*(2), 21–31.

Antikainen, A. (2006). In search of the Nordic model in education. *Scandinavian Journal of Educational Research, 50*(3), 229–243.

Antikainen, A., Harinen, P., & Torres, C.A. (Eds.) (2006). In *From the margins: Adult education, work and civil society*. The Hague: Sense.

Apple, M.W. (2004). *Ideology and curriculum*. 3rd ed. New York: Routledge.

Apple, M.W. (2009). Foreword. In C.A. Torres (Ed.) *Globalizations and education. Collected essays on class, race, gender, and the state*. (pp. ix–xix). New York: Teachers College Press-Columbia University.

Archibugi, D. (1998). Principles of cosmopolitan democracy. In D. Archibugi, D. Held, & M. Köhler (Eds.) *Re-imagining political community*. (pp. 198–228). Cambridge: Polity.

Arnove, R. (1986). *Education and revolution in Nicaragua*. New York: Praeger.

Arnove, R. (2013). Introduction: Reframing comparative education: The dialectic of the global and the local. In R. Arnove, C.A. Torres & S. Franz (Eds.) *Comparative education. The dialectic of the global and the local*. (pp. 1–20). Lanham, Maryland: Rowman and Littlefield.

Arnove, R.F., & Torres, C.A. (1995). Adult education and state policy in Latin America: The contrasting cases of Mexico and Nicaragua. *Comparative Education, 31*(3), 311–325.

Baez, B., & Boyles D. (2009), *The Politics of Inquiry Education Research and the "Culture of Science."* Albany, New York.

Barreiro, J. (1974). *Educación popular y proceso de concientización*. [Popular education and the process of conscientization]. Buenos Aires: Siglo XXI.

Beetham, D. (1993). Liberal democracy and the limits of democratization. In D. Held (Ed.) *Prospects for democracy*. (p. 55) Cambridge: Polity Press.

Benavot, A., Cha, Y.K., Kamens, D., Meyer, J., & Wong, S.Y. (1991). Knowledge for the masses: World models and national curricula, 1920–1986. *American Sociological Review, 56*(1).

Berman, E.H., Marginson, S., Preston, R., & Arnove, R.F. (2007). The political economy of educational reform in Australia, England, and the United States. In R.F. Arnove, & C.A. Torres (Eds.) *Comparative education: The dialectic of the global and the local*. (3rd ed.) (pp. 217–256). Lanham, Maryland: Rowman and Littlefield.

Blaug, M. (1966). Literacy and economic development? *The School Review, 74*(4), 393–415.

Boff, L. (2008, November 12). ¿Está por llegar lo peor de la crisis? [Is the worst of the crisis yet to come?] Newspaper Página 12.

Bonnett, M. (2003). Retrieving nature: Education for a post-humanist age. *Journal of Philosophy of Education, 37*(4), 551–730.

Bouchard G., & Taylor, C. (2008). *Building the future. A time for reconciliation*. Québec: Commission de Consultation Sur Les Pratiques d'accommodement reliées aux différences culturelles.

Bourdieu, P. (2001). "O Neoliberalismo é como a sida." Interview by Romain Leick. *Diário de Notícias*, p. 18, 21 July 2001.

Bunch, C. (2001). Women's human rights: The challenges of global feminism and diversity. In M. Dekoven, (Ed.) *Feminist locations: Global and local, theory and practice*. New Brunswick: Rutgers University Press.

Burbach, R. (2001). *Globalization and postmodern politics: From Zapatists to high-tech robber barons*. London: Pluto Press.

Burbules, N.C., & Torres, C.A. (2000). Globalization and education: An introduction. In N.C. Burbules, & C.A. Torres (Eds.) *Globalization and education: Critical perspectives*. (pp. 1–26). New York: Routledge.

Burke, P.J., & Jackson, S. (2007). *Reconceptualizing lifelong learning: Feminist interventions*. London and New York: Routledge.

Butler, J. (2005). *Giving an account of oneself*. New York: Fordham University Press.

Candy, P.C. (1990). Repertory grids: Playing verbal chess. In J. Mezirow and associates (Eds.) *Fostering critical reflection in adulthood: A guide to transformative and emancipatory learning*. San Francisco: Jossey-Bass.

Carnoy, M. (1999). *Globalization and educational reform: What planners need to know*. Paris: UNESCO/IIEP.

Carnoy, M. (2001). El impacto de la mundialización en las estrategias de reforma educativa. [The impact of globalization on education reform strategies] *Revista de Educación* (número extraordinario), 101–110.

Carnoy, M., & Levin, H. (Eds.) (1985). *Schooling and work in the democratic state*. Stanford, CA: Stanford University Press.

Carnoy, M., & Samoff, J., with M.A. Burris, A. Johnston, & C.A. Torres. (1990). *Education and social transition in the Third World*. Princeton: Princeton University Press.

Castells, M. (1996). *The rise of the network society* (The Information Age: Economy, Society and Culture, Vol. 1). Malden, MA: Blackwell.

Castells, M. (1997). *The power of identity* (The Information Age: Economy, Society and Culture, Vol. 2). Malden, MA: Blackwell.

Castells, M. (1998). *End of millennium* (The Information Age: Economy, Society and Culture, Vol. 3). Malden, MA: Blackwell.

Chrabolowsky, L. (2003). Engendering trade unions and social movements: New proposals of social inclusion in Argentina. Paper presented to the meeting Women and Unions: Still the Most Difficult Revolution, School of Industrial and Labor Relations, Cornell University, November 21–23.

CMMAD. (1988). *Nosso futuro comum*. [Our common future]. Comissão Mundial sobre Meio Ambiente e Desenvolvimento.

Commission of the European Communities. (2007, September 27). Communicaton from the Commission to the Council, the European Parliament, the European Economic and Social Committee, and the Committee of the Regions. Action plan on adult learning. Brussels.

Coombs, Phillips (1968). *The World Educational Crises: A System Analysis*. New York, Oxford University Press.

Cote, M., Day, R.J.F., & de Peuter, G. (Eds.) (2007). *Utopian pedagogy: Radical experiments against neoliberal globalization*. Toronto, Buffalo, and London: University of Toronto Press.

Creppell, I. (1989). Democracy and literacy. *European Journal of Sociology*, 30.

Crowther, J., Johnston, R., Martin, I., & Merrill, B. (2006). Defending the radical margins of university adult Education. In A. Antikainen, P. Harinen, & C.A. Torres (Eds.) In *From the margins: Adult education, work and civil society*. The Hague: Sense Publishers.

Cudworth, E. (2003). *Environment and society*. New York: Routledge.

Dale, R. (2000). Globalization and education: Demonstrating a 'common world education culture' or locating a 'globally structured educational agenda'. *Educational Theory, 50*(4), 427–448.

Dale, R., & Robertson, S. (2003), Editorial Introduction. *Globalisation, Societies and Education, 1*(2).

Daly, K., Schugurensky, D., & Lopes, K. (Eds.) (2009). *Learning democracy by doing: Alternative practices in citizenship learning and participatory democracy*. Toronto: Transformative Learning Centre, OISE/UT.

de Morais, R. (1991). *Educação em tempos oscuros* [Education in dark times]. São Paulo: Autores Asociados-Cortez Editores.

de Sousa Santos, B. (2003). The World Social Forum: Towards a counter-hegemonic globalization. Part of a paper presented at the XXIV International Congress of the Latin American Studies Association, Dallas, March 27–29. Article retrieved from http://www.choike.org/documentos/wsf_s318_sousa.pdf.

Desjardins, R. (2008). Proposal for an ESREA network on policy issues in adult education. Unpublished manuscript. Copenhagen.

Desjardins, R., Rubenson, K., & Milana, M. (2006). *Unequal chances to participate in adult learning: International perspectives.* UNESCO, IIEP.

Deutch, K. (1963). *The nerves of government: Models of political communication and control.* Glencoe, Illinois: The Free Press.

Dewey, J. (1899). *The school and society.* Chicago: University of Chicago Press.

Diarra, M.C. (2008). African Platform Coordinator, African Platform for Adult Education: Civil society report: Forging of partnership towards a renewed vision of adult education in Africa. ANCEFA, ΓΓΜΝΓΤ, ΡΛΛΙ,ΛΓ, ΡΑΜΟΛΛ,

Elkington, J., & Hailes, J. (1988). *The green consumer guide: From shampoo to champagne: High Street shopping for a better environment.* London: Gollanez.

Esping-Andersen, G. (1990). *The three worlds of welfare capitalism.* Cambridge: Cambridge University Press.

Faure, E. et al. (1972). *Learning to be.* Paris: UNESCO.

Fleming, J. (2010) Rethinking Journalism Education. An Examination of News Literacy Initiatives at Stony Brook University. Los Angeles, Graduate School of Education and Information Studies.

Foucault, M. (1991). Governability. In G. Burchell, G. Gordon, & P.M. Miller (Eds.) *The Foucault effect: Studies in governability.* Chicago: The University of Chicago Press.

Foundazione Laboratori Mediterraneo. (1997). Obiettivi e mezzi per il parternariato europeo. [Objectives and goals for the European partnership]. Il Forum Civile EuroMed, Naples, Magma: Foundazionee Laboratorio Mediterraneo.

Fraser, N. (1997). *Justice interruptus: Critical reflections on the "post-socialist condition."* New York: Routledge.

Freire, P. (1968). *Pedagogy of the oppressed.* New York: Continuum.

Freire, P. (1972). *Cultural action for freedom.* New York: Middlesex, Penguin.

Freire, P. (1973). *Education for critical consciousness.* New York: Continuum.

Freire, P. (1987). *A importáncia do ato de ler: em tres artigos que se completam.* [The importance of the act of reading: in threes complementary articles]. São Paulo: Cortez-Autores Associados.

Freire, P. (1993). in conversation with C.A. Torres. Lessons from a fascinating challenge. P. Freire, *Pedagogy of the city.* New York: Continuum.

Freire, P. (1996). *Pedagogia da autonomia: Saberes necessários à prática educativa.* [Pegagogy of autonomy: Necessary knowledge for educational practice]. São Paulo: Paz e Terra.

Freire, P. (1997). *El grito manso. Paulo Freire en la Universidad de San Luis.* [The meek cry. Paulo Freire at the University of San Luis]. Universidad de San Luis, San Luis, Argentina: Siglo XXI.

Freire, P. (1998). *Politics and education.* Trans. by P.L. Wong. Los Angeles, UCLA-Latin American Center Publications, with an introduction by C.A. Torres.

Friedman, T.L. (2006). *The world is flat: The globalized world in the twenty-first century.* New York: Penguin Books.

Furter, P. (1966a). *Educação e reflexão.* [Education and reflection]. Rio de Janeiro: Vozes.

Furter, P. (1966b), *Educação e vida.* [Education and life]. Rio de Janeiro: Vozes.

Gadotti, M. (n/d). La pedagogía de Paulo Freire y el proceso de democratización en el Brasil: Algunos aspectos de su teoría, de su método y de su praxis. [The pedagogy of Paulo Freire and the process of democratization in Brazil: Some aspects of his theory, method and praxis].

Gadotti, M. (n/d). On planetarization and a culture of sustainability and a pedagogy of the Earth. Retrieved from: http://www.paulofreire.org/.

Gadotti, M. (2000). *Pedagogia da terra.* [Pedagogy of the Earth]. Rio de Janeiro: Editorial Peirópolis.

Gadotti, M. (2008). Education for sustainability: A critical contribution to the Decade of Education for Sustainable Development. University of São Paulo-Paulo Freire Institute, São Paulo.

Gadotti, M. (2010). Foro social mundial: Em processo. [World Social Forum: In process]. São Paulo: Paulo Freire Institute website.

Gadotti, M., & Torres, C.A. (Eds.) (1993). *Educación popular: Crisis y perspectivas.* [Popular education: Crisis and perspectives]. Buenos Aires: Miño y Dávila Editores.

Gadotti, M., & Torres, C.A. (Eds.) (1994). *Educação popular: Utopia latinoamericana (ensaios).* [Popular education: Latin American utopia (essays)]. São Paulo: Cortez Editores and Editora da Universidade de São Paulo.

Gadotti, M., & Torres, C.A. (1994). Introdução. Poder e desejo: A educação popular como modelo teórico e como prática social. Editor's Introduction in M. Gadotti & C.A. Torres (Eds.) *Educação popular: Utopia latino-americana (ensaios).* São Paulo: Cortez Editora and Editora da Universidade de São Paulo.

Gadotti, M., & Torres, C.A. (2009). Paulo Freire: Education for development. *Legacies, Development and Change, 40*(6), 1255–1267.

Gitlin, T. (1995). *The twilight of common dreams: Why America is wracked by culture wars.* New York: Herny Hold.

Gohn, Maria. G. (2008). *Novas Teorias dos Movimentos Sociais.* [New Theories of Social Movements]. São Paulo: Edições Loyola.

Gutierrez, F. and Prado, C. (1989) Ecopedagogia e Cidadania Planetaria. São Paulo, Cortez Editores. Preface by Alicia Bárcena.

Habermas, J. (1975). *Legitimation crisis,* edited and translated by Jeremy J. Shapiro. Boston: Beacon.

Habermas, J. (1984). *Theory of communicative action.* London: I. Heinemann.

Habermas, J. 1985. "Psychic Thermidor and the Rebirth of Rebellious Subjectivity." In *Habermas and Modernity,* edited by R.J. Bernstein. Cambridge: MIT University Press.

Hake, B.J. (2006). Late modernity and learning society: Problematic articulations between social arenas, organizations and individuals. In R.V. Castro, A.V. Sancho, & P. Guimarães (Eds.) *Adult education. New routes in a new landscape.* (pp. 31–56). Braga, Portugal: Unit for Adult Education of the University of Minho.

Heaney, T.W., & Horton, A.I. (1990). Reflective engagement for social change. In J. Mezirow and associates (Eds.) *Fostering critical reflections in adulthood: A guide to transformative and emancipatory learning.* San Francisco: Jossey-Bass.

Held, D. (1995). *Democracy and the global order: from the modern state to cosmopolitan governance.* Stanford University Press.

Held, D., & McGrew A. (Eds.) (2000). *The global transformations reader: An introduction to the globalization debate.* (Revised edition, 2007). Malden, MA: Polity Press.

Held, D. (Ed.) (1991). *Political Theory Today.* Stanford: Stanford University Press.

Hernández, C., & Mayur R. (Eds.) (1999). *Pedagogy of the Earth: Education for a sustainable future.* Sterling, VA: Kumarian Press.

Hickling-Hudson, A. (2013) A Theory of Literacies for Considering the Role of Adult and Community Education in Postcolonial Change. In R. Arnove, C.A. Torres & S. Franz (Eds) *Comparative education. The dialectic of the global and the local.* (223–245). Lanham, Maryland: Rowman and Littlefield.

Hinzen, H. (2007). CONFINTEA VI—The UNESCO International Conference on Adult Education in the context of MGDS, EFA, UNLD, LIFE and DESD. Convergence, *40*(3/4), 265–283.

Huntington, S. (1971). Political order in changing societies. New Haven: Yale University Press.

Huttunen, R., & Suoranta, J. (2006). Critical and cultural orientation in radical adult education. In A. Antikainen, P. Harinen, & C.A. Torres (Eds.) *From the margins. Adult education, work and civil society.* The Hague, Sense Publishers.

Huttunen, R. (2008). *Habermas and the problem of indoctrination.* University of Joensuu, mimeographed.

Ianni, O. (1996). *A era do globalismo.* Rio de Janeiro: Civilização Brasileira.

Ianni. O. (1993). *A sociedade global.* Rio de Janeiro: Civilização Brasileira.

Inkeles, Alex & David Smith, (1974). *Becoming Modern.* Cambridge, MA, Harvard University Press.

Illich, I. (1969). *Celebration of awareness: A call for institutional revolution.* Introduction by E. Fromm. Garden City, N.Y.: Doubleday.

Jarvis, P. (1985). *The sociology of adult and continuing education.* London: Croom Helm.

Jenning, B. (2002). *Albert Mansbridge: The life and work of the founder of the WEA.* Leeds: University of Leeds with the Worker's Educational Association.

Jones, L., & Torres, C.A. (2010). The struggle for memory and social justice education: Popular education and social movements reclaiming Latin American civil society. In P. Rose (Ed.) *Achieving Education for All through public-private partnerships?: Non-state provision of education in developing countries.* London: Routledge.

Kellner, D. (2000). Globalization and new social movements: Lessons for critical theory and Pedagogy, In N.C. Burbules & C.A. Torres (Eds.) *Globalization and education: Critical perspectives.* (pp. 299–321). New York: Routledge.

Keogh, H. (2008, September 30). Adult learning and education in the UNESCO region of Europe, North America and Israel. Draft report, unpublished document.

Kettunen, P. (2004). The Nordic model and consensual competitiveness in Finland. In A.M. Castén et al. (Eds.) *Between sociology and history: Essays on microhistory, collective action and nation-building.* Helsinki: SKS.

Knoll, J.H. (2007). The history of the UNESCO international conferences on adult education convergence, *40*(3/4), 21–41.

Knowles, M. (1980). *The modern practice of adult education: From pedagogy to andragogy.* Wilton, CT: Association Press.

La Belle, T. (1986). *Nonformal education in Latin American and the Caribbean: Stability, reform or revolution?* New York: Praeger.

Latapí Sarre, P. (1984). *Tendencias de la educación de adultos en América Latina: Una tipología orientada a su evaluación cualitativa.* [Trends in adult education in Latin America: A typology oriented toward qualitative evaluation]. Pátzcuaro, Mexico: CREFAL.

Lerner, D. (1958). *The passing of the traditional society.* Glencoe, IL: The Free Press.

Lima, L.C. (2010). Do FISC para a CONFINTEA VI, em Belém do Pará associação o direito de aprender. [FISC for CONFINTE VI at Belem, Para. Or the right to learn]. Available at: http://www.direitodeaprender.com.pt.

Lima, L.C. (2010). On the right hand of lifelong education. Unpublished paper presented to a meeting of ICAE, Germany.

Livingstone, D.W. (2004). The learning society: Past, present and future views. R.W.B. Jackson Lecture Centre for the Study of Education and Work, Department of Sociology and Equity Studies in Education, Ontario Institute for Studies in Education of the University of Toronto.

Lohas, Lifestyles of Health and Sustainability. Accessed at www.lohas.com.

Lopez-Ospina, G. (2003). *Planetary sustainability in the age of the information and knowledge society: Working toward 2015 for a sustainable world and future.* Paris: UNESCO.

Luke, A., & Luke, C. (2000). "A Situated Perspective on Cultural Globalization." In *Globalization and Education: Critical Perspectives*, ed. N.C. Burbules and C.A. Torres, pp. 275–97. New York: Routledge.

Mackey, J. (n/d). Creating a new paradigm for business by John Mackey, CEO, Whole Foods Market co-founder, (FLOW).

Mahadevia, D. (2001). Sustainable urban development in India: An inclusive perspective. *Development in Practice, 11*(2).

Mander, J. & Goldsmith, E. (1996). *The Case Against the Global Economy and for a Turn Toward the Local.* San Francisco: Sierra Books.

Marin, A., & Psacharopoulos, G. (1976). Schooling and income distribution. *Review of Economics and Statistics, 58*, 332–338.

Markoff, J. (1986). Literacy and revolt. *American Journal of Sociology, 92*, 323–349.

Martinez, R. (2001, August 5). The ties that bind Latinos, Los Angeles Times, p. M2.

Mayo, P. (2005). *Liberating praxis: Paulo Freire's legacy for radical education and culture.* Westport, CT: Praeger.

Mayo, P. (2008). Competenze e diritto all'apprendimiento: Una concezione alternativa e critica. [The right skills and learning: An alternative conception and criticism]. Unpublished manuscript, Malta.

Mayo, P. (2009). Flying below the radar? Critical approaches to adult education. In M. Apple, L.A. Gandin, & W. Au (Eds.) *Handbook of critical education.* New York and London: Routledge.

Meyer, J., Kamens, D., & Benavot, A. (1992). *School knowledge for the masses: World models and national primary curricular categories in the twentieth century.* Philadelphia: Falmer.

Mezirow, J. (2000). Learning to think like an adult: Core concepts of transformation theory. In J. Mezirow & associates (Eds.) *Learning as transformation: Critical perspective on a theory in progress.* San Francisco, Jossey-Bass.

Milani, C.R.S., & Laniado, R.N. (2006, December 5). Transnational social movements and the globalization agenda: A methodological approach based on the analysis of the World Social Forum. Working Paper 5. The Edelstein Center for Social Research.

Misiaszek, G. W. (2011) Ecopedagogy in the Age of Globalization. Educators' Perspectives of Enviromental Education Programs in the Americas which incorporates Social Justice Education Models. Ph.D. Dissertation, Los Angeles, California, University of California Los Angeles (UCLA)

Morrow, R.A., & Torres, C.A. (1995). *Social Theory and education: A critique of theories of social and cultural reproduction.* Albany, New York: State University of New York Press.

Morrow, R.A. & Torres, C.A. (2004). Gramsci e a educação popular na América Latina. Percepções do debate brasileiro. *Currículo Sem Fronteiras, 4*(2), 33–50.

Mova-Brazil (n/d). See http://www.comminit.com/es/node/69092/37.

Naess, A. (1990). Deep ecology. In A. Dobson (Ed.) *The green reader.* London: André Deutsch.

Nash, K. (2000). *Contemporary political sociology, globalization, politics and power.* Massachussetts and Oxford: Blackwell.

O'Cadiz, M.P., & Torres, C.A. (1994). Literacy, social movements, and class consciousness: Paths from Freire and the São Paulo experience. *Anthropology and Education Quarterly, 25*(3).

O'Cadiz, P.,Wong, P.L., & Torres, C.A. (1998). *Democracy and education: Paulo Freire, educational reform and social movements in Brazil.* Boulder, CO: Westview Press.

O'Connor, J. (1973). *The fiscal crisis of state.* New York: St. Martins Press.

O'Donnell, G., Schmitter, P.C., & Whitehead, L. (1993). *Transitions from authoritarian rule: Latin America.* Baltimore, MD: Johns Hopkins University Press.

OECD (2007) *Understanding the Social Outcomes of Learning.* Paris.

OECD. (2007). *Evidence in education: Linking research and policy.* Paris: OECD.

Ohmae, K. (1990). *The borderless world: Power and strategy in the interlinked world economy.* New York: Harber Business.

Ohmae, K. (1995). *The end of the nation-state: The rise of regional economies.* New York: Free Press.

Olmos, L., Van Heertum, R., & Torres, C.A., (Eds.) (2010). *In the shadows of neoliberal globalization: Educational reform in the last 25 years in comparative perspective.* Oak Park, IL: Bentham Books.

Popkewitz, T.S. (1988). Educational reform: Rhetoric, ritual, and social interest. *Educational Theory, 38*(1), 78–83.

Postma, D.W. (2006). *Why care for nature? In search of an ethical framework for environmental responsibility and education.* New York: Springer.

Psacharopoulos, G. (1988). Critical issues in education and development: A world agenda. *International Journal of Educational Development, 8*(1), 21–26.

Puiggrós, A. (1984). *La educación popular en América Latina.* [Popular education in Latin America] Mexico: Nueva Imagen.

Puiggrós, A. (2005). *De Simón Rodríguez a Paulo Freire, Educación para la integración Iberoamericana.* [From Simon Rodriguez to Paulo Freire: Education for Iberoamerican integration]. Bogotá, Colombia: La Organización Internacional Convenio Andrés Bello.

Razeto Migliaro, L. (1990). *Economia popular de solidaridad: Identidad y proyecto en una vision integradora.* [Popular economy of solidarity: An inclusive view of identity and project]. (2nd edition). Santiago de Chile, Area Pastoral Social de la Conferencia Episcopal de Chile.

Razeto Migliaro, L. (2003). *Le dieci strade dell'economia di solidarietá.* [The ten ways of an economy of solidarity]. Bologna, Italy: EMI.

Rizvi, F. (2006). Imagination and the globalization of educational policy research. *Globalization, Societies and Education, 4*(2), 193–206.

Rhoads, R.A., & Szelényi, K. (2011). *Global Citizenship and the University: Advancing Social Life and Relations in an Interdependent World.* Stanford, CA: Stanford University Press, 2011.

Rhoads, R., & Rhoades, G. (2006). Graduate Student Unionization as a Postindustrial Social Movement: Identity, Ideology, and the Contested US Academy. In Robert Rhoads and Carlos Alberto Torres, *The University, State, and Market. The Political Economy of Globalization in the Americas.* Stanford, California, Stanford University Press, pp. 275–298.

Robertson, S.L. (2003). WTO/GATS and the global education services industry. *Globalization, Societies and education. 1*(3), 259–266.

Rodriguez Brandão, C. (1984). Los caminos cruzados: Formas de pensar y realizar educación en América Latina. *Revista de la Educación de Adultos, 28–41.*

Romão, J.E. (2001). *Globalización o Planetarización. Las Trampas del Discurso Hegemónico.* São Paulo: Instituto Paulo Freire.

Saltzman, C. (2001). "The Many Faces of Activism." In *Feminist Locations: Global and Local, Theory and Practice,* ed. Marianne Dekoven. New Brunswick, Rutgers University Press

Schriever, J. (2004). Multiple internationalities: The emergence of world-level ideology and the persistence of idiosyncratic world- views. Berlin, Humboldt University, Comparative Education Centre, Research Papers, N° 14.

Schugurensky, D., & Torres, C.A. (1994). Adult education and political education: Lessons from comparative, cross-national research in Cuba, México, Nicaragua, and Tanzania. In B. Claussen (Ed.) *Aspects of globalization and internationalization of political education.* Hamburg, Germany: Krämer.

Schuman, H., Inkeles, A., & Smith, D. (1967). "Some social psychological effects and noneffects of literacy in a new nation" *Economic Development and Cultural Change, 16*(1), 1–14.

Scott, P. (Ed.) (1998). *The Globalization of Higher Education.* London: Society for Retired into Higher Education and Open University.

Sen, A. (1999). *Development as freedom.* Oxford: Oxford University Press.

Shor, I. (1992). *Empowering education: Critical teaching for social change.* Chicago: University of Chicago Press.

Shor, I., & Freire, P. (1987). *A pedagogy of liberation: Dialogues on transforming education.* Amherst, MA: Bergin and Garvey.

Shuman, H., Inkeles, A., & Smith, D. (1967). Some social psychological effects and non-effects of literacy in a new nation. *Economic Development and Cultural Change, 16*(1), 1–14.

Slaughter, S., & Leslie, D.L. (1997). *Academic capitalism: Politics, policies, and the entrepreneurial university.* Baltimore: Johns Hopkins University Press.

Soysal, N. (1994). *Limits of citizenship: Migrants and postnational membership in Europe.* Chicago: University of Chicago Press.

Stromquist, N. (2002). *Education in a Globalized World: The Connectivity of Economic Power, Technology, and Knowledge.* Lanham, MD: Rowman & Littlefield.

Teodoro, A., & Torres, C.A. (2007). Introduction. Critique and utopia in the sociology of education. In C.A. Torres & A. Teodoro (Eds.) *Critique and utopia: New developments in the sociology of education.* (pp. 1–8). Lanham, MD, and Boulder, CO: Rowman and Littlefield.

Teodoro, A. (2003). "Educational Policies and New Ways of Governance in a Transnationalization Period." In *The International Handbook on the Sociology of Education,* ed. C.A. Torres and A. Antikainen. Lanham, MD: Rowman and Littlefield.

Teodoro, António (Organizador) *A Educação Superior No Espaço Iberoamericano. Do Elitismo á Trasnacionalização.* Lisbon, Edições Universitarias Lusófona, 2010.

Torres, C.A. (1989). Political culture and state bureaucracy in Mexico: The case of adult education. *International Journal of Educational Development, 9*(1), 53–68.

Torres, C.A. (1990a). *The politics of non-formal education in Latin America.* New York, Praeger.

Torres, C.A. (1990b). Adult education, popular education: Implications for a radical approach to comparative education. *International Journal of Lifelong Education, 9*(4).

Torres, C.A (1991a). A political sociology of adult education: A research agenda. *Education.* University of Malta, *4*(1).

BIBLIOGRAPHY

Torres, C.A. (1991b). The state, non-formal education, and socialism in Cuba, Nicaragua, and Grenada. *Comparative Education Review*, *39*(1), 1–27.

Torres, C.A. (1992a). Estado, políticas públicas e educação de adultos: Entrevista [The state, public policy and adult education: Interview] by Elie Ghanem, CEDI – Centro Ecuménico de Documentação e Informação. São Paulo.

Torres, C.A. (1992b). Participatory action research and popular education in Latin America. *International Journal of Qualitative Studies in Education*, *5*(1).

Torres, C.A. (1992c). The state, nonformal education, and socialism in Cuba, Nicaragua, and Grenada. *Comparative Education Review 35*(1), 191. Translated and published in Spanish by Desarrollo Económico. *Revista de Ciencias Sociales*, *31*(124).

Torres, C.A. (1993a). Adult education as political education: Settings and rationalities in dependent capitalist societies. In M.W. Conley & C.A. Torres (Eds.) *Political education: North American perspectives*. Hamburg, Germany and Paris, France: Kraemer.

Torres, C.A . (1993b). Cultura política de la alfabetizacion. Descripción y análisis de las relaciones entre educación de adultos y sectores populares urbanos en México. [Political culture of literacy: Description and analysis of the relationship between adult education and urban sectors in Mexico]. *Revista Latinoamericana de Estudios Educativos*, 3.

Torres, C.A. (1994a). Adult education for national development. In T. Husén & T.N. Postlethwaite (Eds.) *International Encyclopedia of Education Research and Studies* (2nd ed.). Oxford, England: Pergamon Press.

Torres, C.A. (1994b). Educação de adultos e educação popular na América Latina. [Adult education and popular education in Latin America]. In M. Gadotti & C.A. Torres (Eds.) Educação popular: Utopia latino-americana (ensaios). [Popular education: Latin American utopia]. São Paulo, Brazil: Cortez Editora and Editora da Universidade de São Paulo.

Torres C.A. (1995a). Estado, políticas públicas e educação de adultos. [The state, public policy and adult education]. In M. Gadotti & J.E. Romão (Eds.) Educação de Jovens e Adultos. Teoria, prática e proposta. [Youth and adult education: Theory, practice and proposals]. São Paulo, Brazil: Cortez Editora and Paulo Freire Institute.

Torres, C.A. (1995b). State and education revisited: Why educational researchers should think politically about education. *Review of Research in Education*, *21*, 255–331.

Torres, C.A. (1996). Adult education and instrumental rationality: A critique. *International Journal of Educational Development*, *16*(2), 195–206.

Torres, C.A. (1997a). Adult education for development. In L. Saha & J. Lawrence (Eds.) *International Encyclopedia of Sociology of Education*. Oxford, England: Pergamon.

Torres, C.A. (1997b). Alfabetização e educação de jovens e adultos em países industrializados: Uma reflexão crítica sobre a experiência norte-americana. [Literacy and youth and adult education in industrialized countries: A critical reflection on the North American experience]. *Seminário Internacional Educação e Escolarização de Jovens e Adultos*, 1, Instituto Brasileiro de Estudos e Apoio Comunitário (IBEAC). Brasília, Brazil: Ministério de Educação e do Desporto.

Torres, C.A. (1998a). *Democracy, education and multiculturalism: Dilemmas of citizenship in a global world.* Lanham, MD: Rowman & Littlefield.

Torres, C.A. (1998b). Democracy, education, and multiculturalism: Dilemmas of citizenship in a global world. *Comparative Education Review*, *42*(4), 421–447.

Torres, C.A. (1998c). *Education, power and personal biography: Dialogues with critical educators.* New York: Routledge.

Torres, C.A., (Ed.) (2002a). *La Educación en América Latina.* Buenos Aires: Consejo Latinoamericano de Ciencias Sociales.

Torres, C.A. (2002b). "The State, Privatisation and Educational Policy: A Critique of Neoliberalism in Latin America and Some Ethical and Political Implications." *Comparative Education*, Edited by Robert Cowen (University of London), *38*(4), November, 365–385.

Torres, C. A. (2002c). Globalization, Education, and Citizenship: Solidarity Versus Markets? *American Educational Research Journal* (AERJ), *39*(2, Summer), 363–378.

Torres, C.A. (2003). "Education, Power and the State: Successes and Failures of Latin American Education in the Twentieth Century." In Torres, C.A. and Ari Antikainen, Editors. *The International*

Handbook on the Sociology of Education An International Assessment of New Research and Theory. Lanham, Maryland, Rowman and Littlefield, 256–284.

Torres, C.A. (2004). *La praxis educativa y la acción cultural de Paulo Freire.* [The educational praxis and cultural action of Paulo Freire]. Valencia: Denes Editorial-Edicions del CreC.

Torres, C.A. (2006). *Pedagogia de la Lucha.* [Pedagogy of Struggle]. Valencia: Denes Editorial-Edicions del CReC.

Torres, C.A. (2007a), "Transformative Social Justice Learning: The Legacy of Paulo Freire." In *Utopian Pedagogy. Radical Experiments Against Neoliberal Globalization.* Edited by Mark Cote, Richard J.F. Day, and Greig de Peuter. Toronto, Buffalo, and London, University of Toronto Press, 242–247.

Torres, C.A. (2007b). "The Distorted Worlds of Ivan Illich & Paulo Freire" In Torres, Carlos Alberto and Antonio Teodoro (editors) *Critique and Utopia. New Developments in the Sociology of Education.* Lanham, Maryland: Rowman and Littlefield.

Torres, C.A. (2009a). *Education and globalization.* New York: Routledge.

Torres, C.A. (2009b). *Globalizations and education: Collected essays on class, race, gender, and the state.* New York: Teachers College Press.

Torres, C.A. (2010). "Introdução, La Educación Superior en Tiempos de la Globalización Neoliberal." In António Teodoro (Organizador) *A Educação Superior No Espaço Iberoamericano. Do Elitismo á Trasnacionalização.* Lisbon, Edições Universitarias Lusófona, 11–33.

Torres, C.A. (2011a). Public Universities and the neoliberal common sense: seven iconoclastic theses. *International Studies in Sociology of Education, 21*(3), 177–197.

Torres, CA. (2011b). Dancing on the deck of the Titanic? Adult education, the nation-state and new social movements International. *Review of Education,* Volume 1 / 1955 - Volume 57 /, 39–55.

Torres, C.A., Pannu, R.S., & Kazim Bacchus, M. (1993). Capital accumulation, political legitimation and educational expansion. In J. Dronkers (Ed.) *Education and social change.* Greenwich, CT, and London: JAI Press.

Torres, C.A., & Noguera, P. (Eds.) (2008). *Social justice education for teachers. Paulo Freire and the possible dream.* Rotterdam, The Netherlands: Sense Publishers.

Torres, C.A., & Puiggrós, A. (1995). *The state and public education in Latin America.* Boulder, CO: Westview Press.

Torres, C.A., Romão, J.E., & Teodoro, A. (2012). Redes Institucionais Na América Latina. Construindo as Ciências Sociais e Educação Contemporâneas na América Latina. Los Angeles, São Paulo and Lisbon, manuscript.

Torres, C.A., & Schugurensky. D. (1993a). A comparison of the political economy of adult education in Canada, Mexico and Tanzania. *The Canadian Journal for the Study of Adult Education, 7*(1).

Torres, C.A., & Schugurensky, D. (1993b). La economía política de la educación de adultos desde una perspectiva comparativa: Canada, México y Tanzania. [A comparison of the political economy of adult education in Canada, Mexico and Tanzania]. *Revista Latino-americana de Estudios Educativos, 23*(4).

Torres, C.A., & Schugurensky, D. (1994a). The politics of adult education in comparative perspective: Models, rationalities and adult education policy implementation in Canada, Mexico and Tanzania. *Comparative Education, 30*(2), 131–152.

Torres, C.A., & Schugurensky, D. (1994b). "The Politics of Adult Education in Comparative Perspective: Models, Rationalities, and Adult Education Policy Implementation in Canada, Mexico, and Tanzania." *Comparative Education,* 30(2).

Torres, C.A., & Schugurensky, D. (1995). Therapeutic model of adult education in Canada: Skills and academic upgrading programs in the province of Alberta. *International Journal of Lifelong Education. 4*(2), 144–161.

Torres, C.A., & Schugurensky, D. (1996). A comparison of the political economy of adult education in Canadá, México, and Tanzania. In P. Wangoola & F. Youngman (Eds.) *Towards a transformative political economy of adult education: Theoretical and practical challenges.* DeKalb, IL: LEPS Press.

Torres, C.A., & Antikainen, A. (Eds.) (2003). The International Handbook on the Sociology of Education An International Assessment of New Research and Theory. Lanham, Maryland, Rowman and Littlefield.

UNESCO. (1968a). Literacy work and school education in economic development. In *Readings in the economics of development.* Paris: UNESCO.

UNESCO. (1968b). The conditions of a return to investment in adult literacy development. In *Readings in the economics of development*. Paris: UNESCO.

UNESCO. (1997). The agenda for the future. Hamburg, Germany.

UNESCO. (2005). *World Report: Toward knowledge societies*. Paris: UNESCO Publishing.

UNESCO. (2007). Good practices in the UNECE region. Paris: UNESCO – Education for Sustainable Development in Action. Good Practices N°2.

UNESCO. (2008). Education for All global monitoring report. Paris: UNESCO.

UNESCO. (2009a). Global report on adult learning and education. Hamburg, Germany.

UNESCO. (2009b). The Bélém framework for action. Bélém, Brazil.

Urry, J. (1998). "Contemporary Transformations of Time and Space." In *The Globalization of Higher Education*, ed. P. Scott, 1–17. London: Society for Retired into Higher Education and Open University.

Wallerstein, I. (1997). Social science and the quest for a just society. *American Journal of Sociology, 102*(5), 1241–1257.

Wallerstein, I. (1999). *A left politics for the twenty-first century? or Theory and praxis once again.* Democratie, Fernand Braudel Center, University of New York, Binghamton.

Wallerstein, I. (2005). After developmentalism and globalization, what? *Social Forces, 83*(3), 321–336.

Walther, A. (2006). Regimes of youth transitions: Choice, flexibility and security in young people's experiences across different European contexts. *Young: Nordic Journal of Youth Research, 14*(2), 119–139.

Weiler, H.N. (1983). Legalization, expertise, and participation: Strategies of compensatory legitimation in education policy. *Comparative Education Review, 27*, 259–277.

Went, R. (2000). *Globalization: Neoliberal challenge, radical responses*. London: Pluto Press.

West, C. (1996). *Prophetic thought in postmodern times*. Monroe, Maine: Common Courage Press.

AFTERWORD

Marcella Milana
Los Angeles
December 5, 2012

My first encounter with Carlos Alberto Torres dates back several years through the reading of his work. His deep intellectual concern for social justice, together with his long-term engagement with radical investigations of the relationship of power, politics, and education, has resulted in an extensive production; a production that has crossed geographical borders. Moreover, C.A. Torres's books have been adopted as textbooks in graduate courses in a variety of countries, while his availability to attend lectures, roundtables, and conferences worldwide has brought him to Europe on quite a few occasions. It was during one of these trips that we first shook hands.

C.A. Torres and I joined the launching meeting of a research network on Policy Studies in Adult Education, under the European Society for Research on the Education of Adults (ESREA). It was 2009. C.A. Torres had just been called to serve the UNESCO Institute for Lifelong Learning as an independent expert for the first *Global Report on Adult Learning and Education* (UNESCO, 2009). In the same year, he had been appointed honorary adjunct professor at the Department of Education at Aarhus University (formerly the Danish School of Education), where I held an associate professorship in adult education. It did not take long for us to share our concern for the relationship between adult education and the State and how it was being re-shaped under contemporary globalization processes.

Torres is widely respected for his scholarly expertise in popular education as it took off and developed in Latin America, with a focus on adult learning and community development. Moreover, in much of his writing he advocates critical pedagogy and social justice as means through which to challenge the relations between power and knowledge in education. Not less important, he was a longtime friend and continues to carry the legacy of late Brazilian educator Paulo Freire, whose personal, political, and scholarly engagement clearly demonstrated how adult education is never neutral but inherently political, a theme that emerges clearly in this book.

I have primarily researched adult education within the European context to understand its potentials and concrete contributions to the formation of democratic citizenship. In doing so, I also have been concerned with patterns of participation in adult education and learning opportunities and how these are interconnected with public policies that condition not only their availability, but also the pedagogical quality and significance of learning opportunities. In recent years I have turned my attention to the ways that adult and lifelong education policies, and related practices, are being framed and reshaped under the effects of globalization, in interaction among a plurality of political actors, including inter-state and international organizations, thus expanding my interest well beyond the European region.

While our common interests laid the foundation for a productive discussion, our diverse data sources and foci of analysis proved rather complementary in enhancing our understandings of the challenges for adult education in the twenty first century. These have been (and still are) discussed at the Graduate School of Education and Information Studies at the University of California-Los Angeles (UCLA), thanks to C.A. Torres' invitations to co-teach a graduate course on Non-formal Education in Comparative Perspectives (2011) and lecture in the International Summer Program (2011, 2012) offered by the Paulo Freire Institute he directs, and more recently, thanks to a Marie Curie Fellowship. This ongoing relation also gave me the opportunity to follow at a rather close distance the making of *Political sociology of adult education*.

In this afterword, I intend to address some of the issues that the above debates have brought to light.

Education vs. Learning: Redefining the Object of Policy, Scholarship, and Practice

In Chapter I, C.A. Torres addresses the need for re-conceptualizing lifelong learning, arguing that "the terminology of the field is subject to much controversy and needs to be retooled carefully" (p. 8). As a matter of fact, in the broader field of education, and adult education in particular, we have seen a radical shift in vocabulary from adult and continuing education to lifelong learning over the past few decades. This is evidenced in the rhetorical emphasis of political discourses as well as in the plethora of scholarly work. The most recent examples include the *International handbook of lifelong learning* (Aspin et al., 2001), now in its second edition (Aspin et al., 2012), and *The Routledge international handbook of lifelong learning* (Jarvis, 2009). While these books use "lifelong learning" as an overarching category to explore the complexity of learning processes in diverse socio-historical and geographical contexts, and across sites and ages, they also acknowledge a more or less silent shift in paradigm. As Kuhn (1996) clearly depicts, a shift in paradigm represents a fundamental alteration in the way we define an object of investigation and how the results of such activity can be interpreted and used. When it comes to adult education, a paradigmatic shift that emphasizes learning (e.g. the outcome dimension) rather than education (e.g. the process dimension) embeds a conscious or unconscious reframing of the set of practices that characterize the object of adult education policy, scholarship, and practice. Accordingly, it is worth interrogating how this shift came about. It is my opinion that Biesta (2006) has provided one of the most convincing accounts to date of this paradigm shift as grounded in changes in education theories and philosophies, as well as in observable societal changes. In particular, he suggests that four interrelated trends have contributed to the move from education to learning. These can be shortly resumed, on the one hand, in the emergence of a constructivist or socio-cultural turn combined with a postmodern turn in educational thinking, and, on the other hand, in empirical observation that more people spend more time and money in learning activities, while we witness "the erosion of the welfare State" and the rise of the market economy (Biesta, 2006, p. 18).

Basically, from a theoretical and philosophical point of view, it is Biesta's (2006) argument that scholarly work, for instance the influential book by Lave and Wenger (1991) *Situated learning*, have paved the way for pushing to the background the teacher-learner relation and/or the knowledge content of such interactions, while bringing to the foreground the activities through which people learn in interaction with others that may or may not include education professionals. This has been paralleled with a loss in appeal of education as a viable project of modernity – a project inherited by the Enlightenment and grounded in philosophical humanism and its creed in the rational autonomous being, hence entangled with a deep concern of what constitutes an "educated" person, thus with the type of practice this entails (*bildung*). This is a project that, from a postmodernist perspective, has failed, as provocatively captured by the catchy title *The end of education* by Neil Postman (1995).

From an empirical point of view, the above changes have been accompanied by an increase in individual investment of time and money by adult and mature learners in "individualized" and "individualistic" learning activities (Field, 2000). While the former refers to the form in which learning takes place, as it occurs in interaction between a person and one or more artifacts; the latter addresses the purpose and content of such learning, which are more often than not limited to the pursuit of individual satisfaction. In addition, Biesta (2006) highlights the changing nature of the State in relation to the rise of the market economy that has brought about a decrease in the redistributive function of the State, however coupled with a modification of the relations between the State and its citizens, now based on economic rather than political terms. C.A. Torres has amply addressed this trend throughout this book by contemplating not only the emergence of but also the crisis of such a "neoliberal State."

Yet, as I have argued elsewhere (Milana, 2012a), at least an additional trend to those above mentioned shall be considered, namely political globalization and the increased influence of inter-state organizations in shifting social imaginaries on the relationship of education, work, and the socio-economic development of nation-states.

Seen in this perspective, transnational and inter-state entities with their own interests in education not only assign to the concept of lifelong learning particular values, meanings and norms about the world that become accepted truths; in doing so, they produce specialized knowledge in a conscious effort to legitimize specific political interests, to set the agenda of what can be discussed, and to influence State policies. Yet State membership in transnational and inter-state entities blurs the boundaries between knowledge production and knowledge appropriation or utilization; and this cautions against ascribing the shift from adult education to lifelong learning policies either to global or to local politics. (Milana, 2012, p. 106)

This trend also entangles the emergence of a "global polity" (Corry 2010), or mobilization of a set of social actors, toward the governance, specifically, of adult education. Accordingly, adult education has been made an explicit subject of political action based on de-territorialized norms (cf. Milana, Milana, 2012b). This is evidenced, for instance, by UNESCO's CONFINTEAs, gathering representatives from governments, academia, other transnational entities, including non-governmental organizations, and civil society more broadly. This set of social actors jointly sign recommendations, declarations, and frameworks for future action in the field of adult education worldwide. Similar evidence is found in policy briefs, reports, and cross-national studies promoted by the OECD, with the voluntarily participation of its members, or in more recent communications, conclusions and resolutions by the EU's joint institutions, representing its member states (Council of the European Union), citizens (European Parliament), and the EU as a sovereign body (European Commission), which result from wide consultations among a variety of social actors within and across member states. Still, much empirical research on adult education is still locked in a "nation-state, policy-as-government paradigm" (Ball, 2012, p. xii).

THEORETICAL AND METHODOLOGICAL TOOLS TO RESEARCH 'GLOBAL' ADULT EDUCATION POLICY

Taking as a point of departure that adult education is no longer just a State affair, but has mobilized a set of social actors in its governing, I now shortly discuss some theoretical and methodological parameters to study "global" adult education policy.

Public Policy and Values Permeability

Traditional accounts of public policy contend that governments are faced with social problems to which they should react by identifying the best possible solutions, and believe that government intervention is not only desirable but also necessary to increase national economic and social growth through redistributive measures (Simon 1961; Bardach 1981). Over time this approach showed its limitations for several reasons, among them its failure in delivering generalizable and predictable policy knowledge and outcomes (Wagner, 2007), thus it was replaced by a "structured interactionist" approach that, although still anchored in a similar understanding of policymaking as a rational instrumental process, acknowledges the existence of competing views (Lindblom, 1980; Wildavsky 1979). It was during the 80s and more prominently in the 90s, however, that a different tradition to understanding public policy emerged. This tradition, generally addressed as "post-positivist," interprets public policy as a "social construction" that is spatially and temporally determined, thus it questions the alleged value neutrality of public policy (Bacchi, 2009). In line with this argument, for instance, it has been noted that Keynesian economic theories, which used to structure much of public policy in the past, in the 80s and 90s had lost their appeal for governments under the new inspiration of market ideologies framed by neoliberal thinking (Rizvi & Lingard, 2010). Within this context, "the proliferation of sub-national discourses that dispute the authority of the nation-state, disrupt commonplace understandings of the nation-state as the natural scale of politics" (Ozga et al, 2006, p. 5). A de-naturalisation of the authority of the nation-state, however, does not deny that the regulatory functions of the State still hold.

By applying a post-positive approach to public policymaking, adult education policies within national contexts shall be seen, theoretically, as social constructs that authoritatively allocate country specific values. These constructs depend on and condition the way social problems experienced within a nation are identified and addressed. However, through the complex relations that State officials hold with a variety of political agents within and outside governmental structures, the framing of social problems as well as governmental responses are permeable to global ideologies and imaginaries. Acknowledging these relations implies, from a methodological viewpoint, unlocking adult education policy research from a "State paradigm," which delimits the study of education policy to only some of the places in which it is currently being done.

A Strategic-Relational Approach to the State and Agents' Positionalities

A review of recent theories of the State, as Pierson (2004, p. 77) has observed, although not exempt from controversies, highlights at least a greater historical sensitivity, with their acknowledgement of the uniqueness and contingency of particular State formations, as well as awareness of the complex relation between State and society. Against this background, the traditional definition of the State as an "organized political power" still holds true, however, the organizational means and modality through which it exercises such power in diverse societies is always the resultant of contingent factors and global forces. Poulantzas (1978), for instance, refuses the reductionist interpretation that the State is simply subordinated to the logic of capital or an instrument for class struggle and suggests that, as an "institutional ensemble," the State has no power in itself. State power results from the balance of social forces that act within and upon such an ensemble, and which depends on particular institutional forms. Further elaboration of the State as a "complex social process in and through which specific institutional orders and their broader social preconditions are secured" (Jessop 1990, p. 5) can be found in Jessop's (1990, 2002, 2007) distinctive "strategic-relational" approach. From this perspective, the State is always the result of the balance of social forces that are spatially and timely situated. This implies that the differential capacity of political agents to pursue their own interests within a time horizon is dependent on the complex relation between the strategies these agents adopt and specific State structures, rather than embedded in the State system. Thus the State cannot be reduced to an autonomous actor in relation to others, as its action is determined by the very nature of the broader social relations in which it is situated. In line with this argument, the State represents at the same time the site, the generator, and the product of "strategic selectivity." As a site of strategic selectivity, any given State's type, form, or regime is more or less accessible to certain political agents, and not to others, depending on the strategies these agents adopt to gain power. As a generator of strategic selectivity, politicians and State officials adopt strategies to impose some kind of unity or coherence on State's activities. Finally, as a product of strategic selectivity, any given State's type, form, or regime always results from past political strategies and struggles, thus current political strategies embed past patterns of strategic selectivity as well as their reproductive or transformative potentials (Jessop 1990, 2007).

In his latest work, Jessop (2007) combines the dialogical relation between structure and agency with that of ideation and materiality, recognising the relevance of discursive selectivity in the pursuit of strategic selectivity. From this perspective, the emergence, selection, retention, contestation, and replacement of discourses, although based on social imaginaries, always resonates to a certain extent with the agents' material experience, thus providing cognitive templates that interact with strategic selectivity at the intersection of structural constrain and conjunctural opportunities.

By applying a strategic-relational perspective to the State, State power and action are the resultants of strategic and discursive selectivity by diverse political agents, thus policy processes (as well as their effects) are always contingent, and subject to negotiation and coordination that takes place at individual, organizational, and inter-systemic scales. Accordingly, I contend that forms and mechanisms through which States participate in the activity of inter-state organizations (as well as the effects of such participation) are spatially and temporally determined by strategic and discursive selectivity. Accordingly, membership in inter-state organizations can act as a conjunctural opportunity for (member) states to (re)gain (national) legitimate authority, at the same time as it can act as a structural constraint, in favor of inter-state organizations acting as state-like institutions (i.e. EU, UNESCO, OECD). State-like institutions define or implement collective decisions affecting member states, and their relative populations, in the name of a shared (inter-state) common interest. From a judicial perspective, even when ratified by member states on a voluntarily basis, these decisions still represent a formal agreement binding its signatories to cross-national cooperation (Reinalda & Kulesza, 2006).

Methodologically, this invites us to consider the positionality of countries in inter-state organizations that do policy work in the field of adult education by looking at factors such as the exchange of economic resources, the assignation of responsibilities to State officials within inter-state organizations or of staff from these organizations within national governments, continuity and ruptures in communications among governments and inter-state organizations over time, etc.

Policy Sociology, the Anthropology of Policy and the Re-Bordering of the Research Field

The scenario depicted above has led several scholars to re-define how (public) education policy can be understood and studied, thus Ozga (1987) argues for a "policy sociology ... rooted in the social science tradition, historically informed and drawing on qualitative and illuminative techniques" (p. 1444). Others comply with this claim, however stressing ways in which globalization processes affect public policy. Rizvi and Lingard (2010), for instance, argue that while old accounts of policy processes may still hold useful, these processes are now framed globally and beyond the nation-state, though differently articulated in nationally specific terms. Accordingly, in the authors' view, policy sociology should not only describe power relations and processes through which policies are developed and allocated, but also point at strategies for progressive change that challenge oppressive structures and practices. Yet as Ozga (2000) contends, "policy is to be found everywhere in education, and not just at the level of central government" (p. 2), thus investigations of public policy should also take into account broader policy interpretations, mediations, and enactments in a variety of "policy settings," namely "places, processes and relationships where policy is made" (Ozga, 2000, p. 1), which include, but are not limited to, governments.

Policy anthropology shares similar assumptions. Levinson, Sutton and Winstead (2009), for instance, comply with a definition of policy that goes beyond a written text, stressing the volition, or policy will, of a multiplicity of actors. Specifically, they speak of "appropriation" to depict the process of creative policy interpretation in which a variety of actors with policy volition engage in their everyday practice. Similarly to Levinson at al. (2009), Shore, Wright and Però (1997) define a policy as socially and culturally embedded within domains of meanings at the same time as it reflects those meaning. However, they take distance from more traditional top-down or bottom-up approaches to policy by introducing the concept of "policy worlds," which encapsulate political processes that occur in different sites through the interactions of diverse agents, concepts, and technologies, and generate, consolidate, (and sometime resist) new forms of governance. Accordingly, they argue that any policy can be interpreted, theoretically, as possessing agency, or a complex social life in which it interacts with people, institutions, and other artefacts. In this line of argument while it is not always possible to trace back to an authoritative choice or agent, nor all policy actors involved, it is still possible to make a policy an entry point or lens through which to investigate relations of power and governance, by looking at the links among agents, institutions, discourses, and material practices.

Thus, while a policy sociology perspective conceptualizes policy as a process initiated well before the production of a text (or artifact) that has material and discursive effects on those who are governed through such processes, anthropology of policy assigns agency to policy. Both approaches have important methodological implications for research in adult education as they invite closer investigations of power relations and forms of governance using a policy as an entry point, and suggest at least two analytical categories that, despite their fluidity, can guide the research. These are the "policy setting" (Ozga, 2000) and the "policy world" (Shore at al., 1997). While the former captures a combination of places, processes, and interactions through which policy comes to life, the latter crosses different (geographical) sites and political issues, to capture the interactions of diverse agents, concepts, and technologies. Both categories prove fruitful in moving beyond the "nation-state, policy-as-government paradigm" when researching "global" adult education policy.

To Conclude

Let me now turn to this book, which raises the fundamental question: "What is left if adult education has lost its transformative and empowering vision and mission, and why did it happen?" (p. 20). In answering this question, C.A. Torres brings to light a set of rationalities for public policy in adult education that led to diverse ideal-types of State models. A set of rationalities that, although not exhaustive, points at ways in which not only conceptual developments within the humanities but first and foremost within policy discourses set the agenda of what can be discussed, which questions can be asked, and which answers can be provided when it comes to adult and continuing education policy and practice worldwide, as I have made the case in the preceding sections.

I interpret C.A. Torres' approach as an invitation to bold scholarship that resists taken-for-granted assumptions as the only possible "consciousness of belonging across the world-time and world-space" (Steger, 2009). The main argument he puts forward in this book is to look at the crises of modern civilization as the bigger picture that can open a "window for alternative rationalities in adult education" (p. 39).

According to common sense, "crisis" points at a social event of unstable nature that often occurs abruptly, and is usually deemed to bring about negative changes, or at least uncertainty about established conditions. C.A. Torres seems to suggest a different way of looking at and interpreting these crises. When we draw on its original Greek etymology, "crisis" refers to judgment, power of distinguishing, decision, choice, etc, thus emphasizing its qualitative aspect that is either subjectively or objectively, for or against. In line with this perspective, a crisis represents a crucial, decisive situation, a turning point that can lead to a positive change in due time. In psychology, a crisis can bring positive changes in a person's life. In a drama, the crisis represents the peak of a conflict that is finally resolved. Thus it is worth interrogating under which conditions the crises of modern civilization could bring about a positive change and finally resolve the peak of the conflict that contemporary globalization processes have brought about in the field of adult education.

With this book, C.A. Torres brilliantly does so; hence creating a space for affirmative action not by politicians, technocrats, or bureaucrats but by scholars (and practitioners) who comply with the "untested feasibility" advocated by Paulo Freire as a guiding principle for their work. The concept refers to a combination of a personal belief "that the world is not in a state of being that can be taken for granted, and that a different world may be dreamt about," however combined with "the idea of agency and possibility, meaning that another world is not only desirable but also possible" (Schugurensky, 2011, p. 74).

C.A. Torres "stands up for adult education" by claiming for a political sociology to examine adult education systems, organizational processes, institutional dynamics, rules, and regulations – including prevailing traditions and customs, however intertwined with a pedagogical perspective rooted in an epistemology that favors critical consciousness. Such an epistemology recognizes that all human interactions and experiences involve power relations; therefore it shall always be subject to constant questioning and systematic critique. In other words, it is an epistemology that refuses reducing adult education to vocational and work-based education, while expanding it to support a sense of community across culture, race, gender, and geographical territories. In short, his is an epistemology that problematizes the relationship between society and the environment, and re-appropriates adult education as a public sphere of deliberation rather than a good in exchange for money.

If we take C.A. Torres's invitation seriously as scholars, we are called upon to establish new research agendas that investigate the effects of globalization on adult education and the relations between transnational policymaking and state models that are conditioned by different types of structural forces – ranging from power relations among different interest groups, economic relations between foreign aid donors and recipients, the functioning and role of the State, etc.

In ending this afterword, I would like to raise few questions that may guide future research in adult education: Which structural forces frame what counts as adult education? How do they delimit or increase the State's maneuver in this field? Who makes policies at the global level? How are these policies remade through local implementation? And last but not least: What are the implications in very different contexts? How do they help to reduce the North-South divide?

REFERENCES

Aspin, D.N., Chapman, J., Evans, K., & Bagnall, R. (Eds.) (2012). *Second international handbook of lifelong learning*. Dordrecht: Springer.

Aspin, D.N., Chapman, J., Hatton, M., & Sawano, Y. (Eds.) (2001). *International handbook of lifelong learning*. Dordrecht: Springer.

Bacchi, C. (2009). *Analysing policy: What's the problem represented to be?* Frenchs Forest, NSW: Pearson Australia.

Ball, S.J. (2012). *Global education inc. New policy networks and the neo-liberal imaginary*. New York: Routledge.

Bardach, E. (1981). Problems of problem definition in policy analysis. In J.P. Crecine (Ed.). *Research in public policy analysis* (Vol. 1, pp. 161–171). Greenwich, Conn: JAI Press.

Biesta, G.J.J. (2006). *Beyond learning: Democratic education for a human future*. Boulder, Colorado: Paradigm Publishers.

Corry, O. (2010). What is a (global) polity? *Review of International Studies, 36,* 157–180.

Field, J. (2000). *Lifelong learning and the new educational order.* Stoke-on-Trent: Trentham Books.

Jarvis, P. (Ed.) (2009). *The Routledge international handbook of lifelong learning.* New York: Routledge.

Jessop, B. (1990). *State theory: Putting the capitalist state in its place.* Cambridge: Polity.

Jessop, B. (2007). *State power: A strategic-relational approach.* Cambridge: Polity.

Jessop, B. (2002). *The future of the capitalist state.* Cambridge: Polity.

Kuhn, T.S. (1996). *The structure of scientific revolutions.* Chicago and London: University of Chicago Press.

Lave, J., & Wenger, E. (1991). *Situated learning: Legitimate peripheral participation.* Cambridge: Cambridge University Press.

Levinson, B.A.U., Sutton M., & Winstead T. (2009). Education Policy as a Practice of Power: Theoretical Tools, Ethnographic Methods, Democratic Options. *Educational Policy, 23*(6), 767–795.

Lindblom, C.E. (1980). *The policy-making process.* New York: Prentice Hall.

Milana, M. (2012a). Political globalization and the shift from adult education to lifelong learning. *European Journal for Research on the Education and Learning of Adults, 3*(2), 103–117.

Milana, M. (2012b). Globalization, transnational policies and adult education. *International Review of Education.* doi: http://dx.doi.org/10.1007/s11159-012-9313-5

Ozga, J. (1987). Studying education policy through the lives of the policy makers: an attempt to close the macro-micro gap. In S. Walker and L. Barton (Eds.), *Changing policies, changing teachers: new directions for schooling?* Milton Keynes: Open University Press.

Ozga, J. (2000). *Policy research in educational settings contested terrain.* Buckingham: Open University Press.

Ozga, J., Seddon, T., & Popkewitz, T.S. (Eds.). Education Research and policy: steering the knowledge-based economy (World Yearbook of Education 2006). New York and London: Routledge.

Pierson, C. (2004). *The modern state* (2nd ed.). London/New York: Routledge.

Postman, N. (1995). *The end of education: Redefining the value of school.* New York: Knopf.

Poulantzas, N. (1978). *State, power, socialism.* London: Verso.

Reinalda, B., & Kulesza, E. (2006). *The Bologna process – Harmonizing Europe's higher education (2. revised edition).* Leverkursen, Germany: Barbara Budric Piblisher.

Rizvi, F., & Lingard, B. (2010). *Globalizing education policy.* New York: Routledge.

Schugurensky, D. (2011). *Paulo Freire.* Continuum.

Shore, C., Wright, S., & Però, D. (Eds.) (1997). *Policy worlds: Anthropology and analysis of contemporary power.* London: Routledge.

Simon, H.A. (1961). Decision making and planning. In H.S. Perloff (Ed.), *Planning and the urban community.* Pittsburgh: Carnegie Institute of Technology and the University of Pittsburgh Press.

Steger, M.B. (2009). *Globalization. A brief insight.* New York: Sterling.

UNESCO (Institute for Lifelong Learning). (2009). *Global report on adult learning and education.* Hamburg: Author.

Wagner, P. (2007). 'Public policy, social science, and the State'. In F. Fischer, G.J. Miller, and M.S. Sidney (Eds.), *Handbook of Public Policy Analysis: Theory, Politics, and Methods.* London: Taylor and Francis.

Wildavsky, A. (1979). *Speaking truth to power: The art and craft of policy analysis.* Boston: Little Brown and Company.

PRAISE FOR THE BOOK-BACK JACKET

"If we think of those who have linked adult education with the aspirations for truly equitable, democratic and participatory politics, we think of Richard Tawney and the Fabian Socialists, of Raymond Williams and birth of cultural studies, and Paulo Freire and the celebration of the power of all ordinary people to create new knowledge of transformation and to name the world. With this book, the best book in my opinion from one of our most prolific scholars, we add the name of Torres to those whose words leap from the page and into the strategies of possibility. Bravo."

Budd L Hall
Co-Chair, UNESCO Chair in Community-Based Research and Social
Responsibility in Higher Education
University of Victoria, BC, Canada

"This book offers a word of critique but also one of hope. In our dispiriting era, Torres provides a cogent political sociology of adult learning and education, based on a Freirian critical theory. Yet, the author also provides an inspiring perspective on how not-taken-for granted realities can be reverted by new social movements and critical public intellectuals, which does fill scholars and educators with hope."

Massimiliano Tarozzi
Department of Cognitive Sciences and Education
University of Trento

"Adult learning and education systems are potential corridors of communication that have the potential to link various spheres of life and subsystems of human activity… and to do so in more socially just ways. Our societies have yet to figure out how to develop these systems to achieve such a feat. This book is at the forefront of synthesizing what we need to know to make it happen."

Richard Desjardins, OECD. Paris.

Adult education serves many sometimes contradictory purposes–for example, skill development, self realization, and political empowerment. In this lucid book, Torres shows how these multiple purposes reflect different understandings of the political subject, the state, and the possibilities and meaning of social change in our neoliberal moment. The reader is left with a powerful vision of adult education of, by, and for social justice.

Professor John Rogers, UCLA

Through the rich insights of a political sociology of education, Carlos A. Torres provides a cutting-edge analysis of the systems and structures that currently shape and constrain adult education but also of the ways we might reconceptualise and reformulate those systems and structures for liberatory and democratic possibilities. At a time when we are in urgent need to re-engage our pedagogical imaginations for social justice education, this seminal book offers precisely the nourishment required to refuel our intellectual, critical and creative capacity to dream of and develop more equitable, reflexive and transformative educational spaces.

Penny Jane Burke
Professor of Education and Director of Paulo Freire Institute-UK
University of Sussex

INDEX

CPSIA information can be obtained
at www.ICGtesting.com
Printed in the USA
LVOW13s2331171116

513510LV00005B/22/P